Contents

6	Time Line Of The Saxon & Viking Period	
7	Introduction	
10	Styles Of Art	
12	Notes For Collectors	
17	Chapter 1	Buckles
22	Chapter 2	Strap Ends
29	Chapter 3	Cruciform, Long & Equal-Arm Brooches
40	Chapter 4	Disc Brooches
52	Chapter 5	Annular & Plate Brooches & Dress Pins
60	Chapter 6	Keys, Spoons, Hanging Bowl & Casket Mounts
72	Chapter 7	Jewellery & Beads
78	Chapter 8	Stirrup Mounts & Harness Fittings
84	Chapter 9	Weights & Gaming Counters
92	Runes	
93	Chapter 10	Wrist-Clasps & Dress Hooks
98	Chapter 11	Sword & Scabbard Fittings, Knives & Weapons
104	Genealogical Chart Of The Norse Gods	
106	Select Bibliography	

Editor
Greg Payne

Author
Nigel Mills

Published by
Greenlight Publishing
The Publishing House
119 Newland Street
Witham, Essex CM8 1WF
Tel: 01376 521900
email: info@greenlightpublishing.co.uk

Printed by
Buxton Press, Derbyshire

ISBN 1 897738 05 6

© 2012 Greenlight Publishing

All right reserved. No part of this publication may be reproduced, stored in a retrieval system, or transmitted in any form by any means, electronic, mechanical photocopying, recording or otherwise, without the prior permission of Greenlight Publishing.

For other great books visit: www.greenlightpublishing.co.uk

Other Books by the Same Author

Roman Artefacts - first published 1995
ISBN 1 897738 07 2 (out of print)

Medieval Artefacts - first published 1999
ISBN 1 897738 27 7

Celtic & Roman Artefacts - first published 2000
ISBN 1 897738 37 4

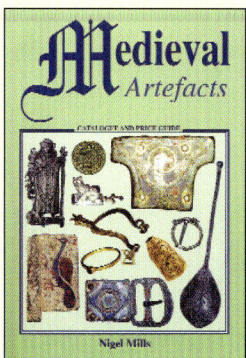 

Available from: Greenlight Publishing,
119 Newland Street, Witham, Essex CM8 1WF
Tel: 01376 521900

A thousand years ago in the churches and monasteries was heard the prayer: "From the wrath of the Northmen, O Lord deliver us." This prayer was amply justified. The Northmen were the Vikings: Danes Norwegians, and Swedes, whose plunderings ranged from private acts of piracy and coastal raids to formidable invasions in the quest of new lands to colonise. Viking activity started before A.D. 800, and more than two centuries elapsed before it ceased.

The Vikings by Johannes Brondsted

Time Line Of The Saxon & Viking Periods

AD 400-2	Withdrawal of part of Roman garrison forces by Flavius Stilicho
406	Britain revolts from Honorius
407	Constantine III proclaimed in Britain
409	Britain revolts from Constantine III and end of Roman rule in Britain
410	Honorius writes to the *civitates* of Britain
411	Constantine III killed
429	Visit of St. Germanus to Britian
c425-55	Reign of Vortigern
c453	Hengest and Horsa settle in Kent
c455	Hengest rebels against Vortigern
c477	Saxon settlement of Sussex
c495	Saxon settlement of Wessex
c500	Battle of Mons Badonicus
560	Aethelberht becomes king in Kent
577	West Saxons capture Gloucester, Cirencester, and Bath
597	St. Augustine converts Aethelbert of Kent
616	Raedwald of East Anglia, as over-king, makes Edwin king of Northumbria
627	Conversion of Edwin
633	Battle of Heavenfield, Oswald of Northumbria becomes over-king
635	Conversion of Cynegils of Wessex
642	Oswald is killed at Oswestry by Penda of Mercia
655	Penda is killed at the Winwaed by Oswy of Northumbria, who becomes over-king
664	Synod of Whitby
672	Battle of the Trent, and the start of the rise of Mercia
685-688	Expansion of Wessex under Caedwalla taking in Kent, Surrey and Sussex
716	Accession of Aethelbald in Mercia
731	Bede completes his "Ecclesiastical History"
735	Death of Bede
757	Death of Aethelbald. Offa becomes king of Mercia
793-5	Danish raids on Lindisfarne, Jarrow, and Iona
796	Death of Offa
825	Mercians defeated by Egbert of Wessex at Wroughton who annexes Kent, Essex, Surrey, and Sussex
835	Danish raid on Kent
851	Vikings winter in Thanet and attack London and Canterbury
865	Danish Great Army lands in East Anglia
866-7	Danes attack Northumbria
867-8	Danes move into Mercia
870	East Anglia falls to the Danes. Murder of St. Edmund
871	Danes attack Wessex. Alfred becomes king
874	Mercia falls to the Danes
878	Alfred defeats the Danes at Edington and Guthrum is baptised
899	Death of Alfred. Edward the Elder becomes king of Wessex
910-20	Edward and Aethelflaed reconquer most of the Danelaw
919	Norse kingdom of York is founded by Raegnald
924	Death of Edward. Accession of Athelstan
939	Death of Athelstan. Accession of Edmund
946	Death of Edmund
954	The last king of York is deposed
959	Accession of Edgar
975	Death of Edgar. Edward becomes king
979	Murder of Edward. Aethelred the Unready becomes king
991	Danish victory against Alderman Byrhtnoth and Essex levies at Maldon. Treaty between England and Normandy
1002	Aethelred orders the massacre of all Danes in England
1003	Danish invasion led by King Swein
1013	Swein returns and the Danelaw accepts him as king
1014	Swein dies and the Danish army in England elect Cnut as their king
1016	Cnut defeats Edmund at Ashingdon and becomes king of all England
1035	Death of Cnut
1037	Harold becomes king
1040	Death of Harold. Harrhacnut becomes king
1042	Death of Harthacnut. Edward the Confessor becomes king
1064-5	Earl Harold visits Duke William in Normandy
1066	Death of King Edward, Earl Harold becomes king. In September King Harold of England defeats and kills King Harald of Norway at Stamford Bridge. In October Duke William of Normandy defeats and kills King Harold of England at Hastings. In December William is consecrated king.

Introduction

The first reference to Saxon raids on Britain was in AD 286, when the naval commander (and later usurper) Carausius was employed to stop the pirates who were operating in the North Sea. These raids continued throughout the 4th century.

The Roman Occupation of Britain came to a dramatic end in AD 410 when the Emperor Honorius answered to a plea for help from the Province with the statement that the Britons were to defend themselves. It is difficult to know how quickly the Roman traditions disintegrated, but during the 5th century Britain returned to its pre-Roman Celtic warrior society. The Welsh language was more widely spoken than Latin and the supply of Roman coinage dried up. The silver coins already in circulation became severely clipped, and barbarous imitations of Roman gold coins were used.

During the 5th century Britain was ruled by tyrants (such as Vortigern) who would have dismantled the Roman towns, replacing stone buildings with timber constructions.

In the west and in the highlands the native Celts continued to hold power. However, by AD 441 the Germanic Saxons, Angles and Jutes ruled the east and south of the country. They had, in turn, been driven westwards from Europe by the Huns. The Anglo-Saxons initially helped to repel the Northern raids by the Picts and Scots, but quickly established permanent settlements and became settler-farmers. The era of King Arthur has been linked to the battle of Mons Budonicus in AD 500, when the Anglo-Saxons were beaten by Britons under a leader still using Roman methods and tactics. From the excavations of burials dating from AD 450-550 paganism replaced Christianity. This is shown by the fact that the dead were buried with their jewellery and weapons for use in the afterlife. The principal pagan war gods at this time were called Tiw and Woden, together with Thor, Frig (a goddess), and the fertility goddess Eostre (Easter). Our knowledge of the 5th century is based on the writings of St.Patrick in Ireland, while in the 6th century information comes from the Welsh monk Gildas. In the late 6th century separate - and rival - Anglo-Saxon kingdoms came into being, each with its own king (basically a successful war lord who had accumulated treasure and lands) and different dialects. There were approximately 12 kingdoms: the Jutes occupied Kent and the Isle of Wight; the Saxons occupied Essex, Sussex and Wessex; the Angles occupied East Anglia; the Hwicce occupied Worcestershire and Gloucestershire; and the north-east was occupied by the Deira and Bernicar.

In AD 597 Benedictine monks led by St. Augustine arrived in Kent on a mission to reintroduce Christianity. In AD 600 St. Augustine became the first Archbishop of Canterbury. In AD 634 Oswald became the king of Northumbria and quickly converted the kingdom fully to Christianity. By the end of the 7th century Christianity was accepted by all the different Anglo-Saxon kings. One possible explanation for this is based on perceived economic and political success linked to the late Roman occupation of Britain when Christianity had taken over from paganism. Monasteries and churches were

Fig1 CM

built all over the country and received substantial donations of land and money from the religion's supporters. As a result, during the 7th and 8th century the Church became extremely wealthy and powerful. Monasteries, especially in Northumbria, became the centres of learning, teaching Latin in schools and producing illuminated manuscripts such as the Lindisfarne Gospels (written circa AD 698). In AD 731 the monk Bede in Northumbria wrote the Ecclesiastical History of the English People.

In the early 7th century the first Anglo-Saxon gold coins were minted in London and in Kent. The Crondall Hoard contained the largest number of gold Anglo-Saxon coins found in Britain (101 *thrymsas* of which 73 were Anglo-Saxon). **Fig1** shows a pale gold shilling or *thrymsa* struck circa AD 660. It is called the Constantine or "oath taking" type and has a diademed bust facing right with a star in annulets in front. On the reverse is a lyre surmounted by two crosses. Unfortunately the coin has fragmented and one third is missing.

Most of the gold *thrymsas* found in Britain are Merovingian in origin

Fig2

and are of varied fineness of gold. They were minted all over Gaul and the legend on the coins includes the name of a moneyer and place of issue. The *thrymsas* gradually became debased with silver (electrum) and by AD 675 were made of just silver and now called *sceats* (but known as *deniers* on the Continent). **Fig2** shows two different Continental Frisian examples. The coin on the left has a helmeted bust facing right with rune-like lettering in front. On the reverse is a cross with TOTI around it. This example dates from AD 695-740. **Fig2** right is a porcupine *sceat* with a standard reverse again with the letters TOTI. These Continental *sceats* circulated all over England and Northern Europe.

Fig3

Many different designs were used for the *sceats* reflecting different kingdoms around the country. **Fig3** shows a facing head on the obverse, and a long-legged quadruped on the reverse possibly intended to be a dog. It is a type assigned to the East Coast of Britain. The weight of *sceattas* in the early 8th century fell from 1.25gm to 1gm in weight, and then became very base silver during the middle of the 8th century. In the 7th and 8th centuries the kings of Northumbria were extending their kingdom, which at this time covered all of northern England above Leeds (from east coast to west coast) and Scotland up to Edinburgh. They also issued their own coins of markedly different style. Aldfrith (685-705) was the first Northumbria king to strike *sceattas* in his own name. These were struck before AD 704 probably in conjunction with his archbishop. Depictions on these coins may be representations of the king or ecclesiastical images. **Fig4** shows a silver *sceat* issued by Eadberht (737-758). On the obverse is a small cross with the king's name and on the reverse a fantastic quadruped with a cross above its back and *triquetra* between its legs.

Fig4

In the south of England (Southumbria) the Mercians dominated in the 8th and early 9th century under the overlords Aethelbald (716-757), Offa (757-796), and Coenwulf (796-821). They controlled the Midlands and annexed Saxon and Jutish kingdoms, taking tributes from all the tribal leaders. Offa was the first Mercian king to issue silver pennies (757-796). Most of these were minted in Canterbury. **Fig5** shows a very finely executed penny of Offa with his portrait facing to the right. On the reverse is a flower of four petals over a plain cross with a crescent in each angle. Around this is the money's name LULUA divided by four bosses.

A tremendous variety of Offa coins exist, some even portraying his wife Cynethryth. There are very few known die duplications, which indicates an extensive issue, under royal control, with the melting down of any foreign coins to cover the growing and prosperous Mercian kingdom. Coin production in Kent was in conjunction with the Archbishop of Canterbury Jaenberht (765-792).

Offa is best remembered for his dyke, built in the late 780s. It was a massive earthwork 25ft deep and

Fig5

60ft across separating the western Mercian border and Wales. After Offa's death a distant cousin Coenwulf became overlord. The word overlord or Bretwalda meant a Briton ruler. **Fig6** shows a non-portrait silver penny of Coenwulf struck in London with an M on the obverse, and on the reverse a *tribrach* between the arms of which is the moneyer's name IBBA.

In 825 the Mercians were defeated by King Ecgberht of Wessex at the

Fig6   CM

Battle of Ellenden, He went on to become the dominant power in the south of Britain.

In AD 793 Lindisfarne, an island monastery off the coast of Northumberland, was attacked by Vikings from Norway. This was to be the beginning of the frequent pillaging of monasteries and raids on coastal towns. By AD 850 Danish Vikings who had been raiding the south of Britain wintered on the Isle of Thanet, and subsequently attacked London and Canterbury. The wealth of England was systematically plundered by the Vikings, melted down, and transported back to Scandinavia.

In the 9th century the four main kingdoms of England comprising Northumbria, East Anglia, Mercia, and Wessex were largely overrun by Viking invaders, with only Wessex remaining after AD 870.

In AD 876 the Vikings settled in the north and east of England. They established a strong agricultural economy in an area known as the Danelaw, which covered England above a line following Watling Street from Chester to London.

In AD 886 Alfred King of Wessex opposed the Danish Vikings, and recaptured London. He became king of the Anglo-Saxons and produced a code of laws in the 880s, which helped to create a new social order. Alfred also revived religious teaching that had ceased during the Viking expansion.

King Athelstan (AD 924-939), Alfred's grandson, invaded Northumbria in AD 927 and recaptured York from the Vikings. This was followed by successful attacks on Wales and Cornwall. This enabled Athelstan to become the first true ruler of Britain for 500 years. He strengthened royal control with the creation of shires.

A new coinage of silver pennies was introduced by King Edgar in 973, which now included a portrait of the king as a standard obverse. The reverse stated the moneyer and mint name. This was a new golden age.

Viking raids restarted in AD 981 and intensified under Sven Forkbeard in AD 991. Viking attacks continued on southern England despite peace treaties and payments of Danegeld by Aethelred II. In the following 20 years a total of £149,000 in gold and silver was paid to the Vikings.

Fig7 shows the obverse and reverse of two issues of Aethelred II (AD 978-1016). On the left is a helmet type 1003-1009. This shows a bust left in armour with a radiate helmet, and on the reverse a long cross voided over a square with trefoils. The coin was issued by a London moneyer, Godric. On the right is a last small cross type, 1009-1017, with a diademed bust facing left; it was minted in Canterbury by the moneyer Leofnoth. Both of these coins bear "peck-marks" which are knife cuts made by the Vikings to test the purity of silver.

In AD 1016 the king of Denmark Cnut, who was a Christian, became the king of Norway, part of Sweden, and also England. In 1017 he received a Danegeld payment of £72,000.

In 1066 Harold II took the throne of England against the claims of William of Normandy and Harald Hardrada of Norway. Both attacked England within a few weeks, culminating in the victory of William at Hastings and ending the Anglo-Saxon dynasty.

Fig7   CM

Styles of Art

Saxon Forms

Fig8 *(AS166)*

Style I Animal

In 1904, Dr Bernhard Salin in Stockholm established a sequence of zoomorphic designs giving each a specific classification. Style I is the first zoomorphic style and was used in Scandinavian/Germanic art circa AD 475. It was popular in Britain between AD 500-550 and was most widespread in Kent. It is composed of a segmented animal usually with a triple stranded ribbon-like body, sometimes combined with a crouching leg motif with three claws. The rounded head resembles a helmet in form. The heads can be single or doubled (see Fig8).

Fig10 *(AS159)*

Animals With Interlace

This Anglo-Saxon development represents a new style of zoomorphic art referred to on the Continent as "Style III Animal". It dates to the second half of the 8th century and has the distinctive feature of more complex interlaced ribbon-like animal bodies forming a network of loops. A sword pommel of the late 8th century, shows two animals confronting each other with overlapping heads. Each of the bodies and tails are speckled, which is a typical feature of this period. The exact nature of the interlacing design varies in different regions, as do the animals represented - see Fig10 (AS159). This style continued into the early 9th century, and is regarded as the predecessor to the Viking Borre style.

Fig9 *(AS274)*

Style II Animal

This second phase of zoomorphic art emerged AD 560-570, coinciding with the end of the migration period. It was used up until circa AD 650. It was especially popular on gold filigree work at the beginning of the 7th century (see Fig9), but was also used on chip carved and repousse work. It gradually replaced the earlier zoomorphic style, which had become devolved and more simplistic at the middle of the 6th century. It is composed of backbiting interlacing ribbon-bodied animals, with snake-like heads.

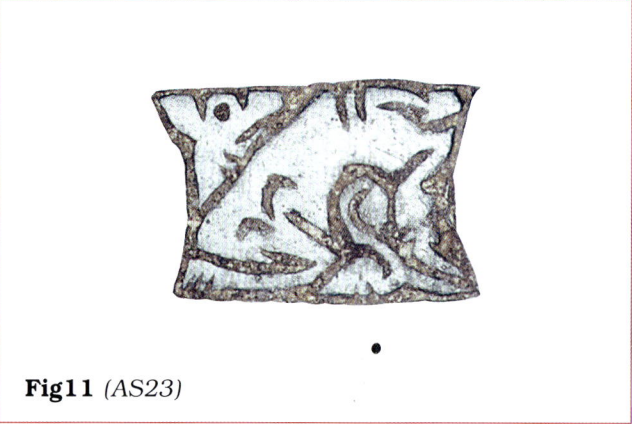

Fig11 *(AS23)*

Trewhiddle Style

In 1774 a collection of silver and gold objects was found inside a silver chalice. The hoard was discovered by tin miners in a stream near St Austel in Cornwall at a depth of 17ft. The pieces included coins of Alfred the Great and King Coelwulf II of Mercia, which dated to circa AD 875. Some of the strap ends and fittings depicted animal designs in a distinctive form now named Trewhiddle (see Fig11). The animals are clearly defined and arranged singly in panels in a grotesque form.

Viking Forms

Fig12 *(V87)*

Borre Style
This was named after a town in Norway where an important set of heavily ornamented gilt bronze mounts were found in a grave. This form of art developed in Scandinavia during the mid 9th century and was introduced to England around AD 865. This makes it the first Scandinavian style to be used in the Viking settlements of northern Britain. The primary design consists of two bands of ribbons bound by a series of rings and lozenges in a geometric configuration forming knots and called a "ring-chain". Additionally, a zoomorphic head appears as a terminal decoration. This is a triangular shaped head with projecting ears and round eyes. It is an Anglo-Scandinavian form of the "gripping beast".

The exact nature of Borre style varies considerably depending on the individual craftsman involved. This style of art was commonly used on strap ends and disc brooches from AD 865 to the mid 10th century. One variety is referred to as the "Borre knot" (see Fig12).

Fig14 *(V168)*

Ringerike Style
This style is named after a particular form of sandstone found at Oslo, which the Vikings used for building. It came to England with the arrival from Denmark of King Cnut in AD 1016. The main art form uses vine scrolls and acanthus leaves as a foliate design. The use of zoomorphic features occur with the limbs of the animals developing or sprouting into tendrils that interlace and intertwine (see Fig14). Sometimes there is a crest on the animal's head or a leaf between animal heads. Ringerike art appeared in a simple form on stirrup mounts and buckles in the 11th century.

Fig13 *(V92)*

Jellinge Style
This is named after a silver cup found in a king's burial at Jelling in Jutland, Denmark. It was introduced to England late in the 9th century and continued to be used into the first half of the 10th century. The designs used are more suited to stonework than metalwork. The main form comprises ribbon-like animals, normally "S" in shape with a rounded head. The bodies of the animals are intertwined and are segmented by straight lines forming a ladder pattern along their length see Fig13. In Britain, this style was also influenced by Anglo-Saxon art.

Fig15 *(V169)*

Urnes Style
This is named after wooden carvings on a stave church at Urnes in Norway. It arrived in England shortly before the Norman Conquest in the mid 11th century and continued into the 12th century. It represents the last of the pagan art forms in Scandinavia and through Christian influence develops into the medieval Romanesque style. The design is normally cast in openwork form, giving a greater depth to the figures. It incorporates curving lines enclosing ribbon-shaped quadrupeds, sometimes entwined, with biting snakes in a "combat motif" (see Fig15). A beast with a protruding head and curving body interlaced with its own limbs and spiral coiled tails, is a common feature of Urnes style.

Notes For Collectors

Many people regard the collecting of antiquities as an eccentric activity, mostly confined to museum curators or historians. In recent years, however, the availability of artefacts - even from the Dark Ages - has been increased due to the popularity of metal detecting. This has encouraged more members of the public to collect antiquities and has engendered an understanding of what is a very complex field. From a personal viewpoint, this period in our history has been the most difficult to fully appreciate as it encompasses the pagan Anglo-Saxons, the Jutes, the Franks, the Merovingians, the pagan Vikings, and finally the Normans. In fact, most collectors specialise in just one particular style of art or object from this diversity of cultures.

If you do decide to collect antiquities it is important to become familiar with, and to understand, the objects in question. Visiting museums, reading archaeological reports, attending antiquity fairs, and calling on dealers are all part of the learning process.

The first question that you have to ask yourself when being offered an artefact is whether the item is genuine. Copies of ancient artefacts have been produced over the last 200 years; some of them are exceedingly well-crafted, while others are little more than tourist souvenirs. Secondly, you have to establish that the surface patina or colour of the item has not been changed from the original. Lastly, you should be sure that no repairs or additions have been made. In some cases these can be contemporary, while the traces of Super Glue indicate a recent alteration. Once you have satisfied yourself to the above conditions, a decision can then be made whether the asking price is reasonable.

My own involvement in excavating artefacts has enabled me to develop an understanding of how objects should look and feel after being buried in the ground for over 1,000 years. The different patinas that develop on bronze can indicate the type of alloy the object was made from, and the environment in which it was discovered. Different countries and regions produce objects showing different, if sometimes subtle, forms of patinas. For example, bronze objects from northern Scandinavian countries have a partial green patina that has been affected by permafrost. This is quite distinctive.

The place of origin of artefacts is quite often changed by the unscrupulous to suit the prevailing market conditions. This is nothing new, and has been going on since collecting of artefacts first became popular. The most important factor to consider is where an item was produced, and then to consider its provenance. For example, is the object Anglo-Scandinavian or Scandinavian in origin? However, the distribution and subsequent usage of artefacts of this period can span many countries.

Forgeries

If an artefact is of high value then a great deal of care and attention will be spent by the dishonest in producing a forgery. It requires only £30 of scrap gold and a day's labour to produce a forgery of a Viking gold ring potentially worth £500-£1,000. Many items of silver jewellery are cast and then toned or re-patinated in order to be sold as originals. The signs to look for on silver objects include a lack of detail and black highlighting. Also, pitting can reveal a poor quality metal and inexpert casting.

Bronze artefacts are more difficult to fake because of the corrosion and patination that develops on the metal over many centuries. It is recommended that magnification through a lens or even with a binocular microscope is used to inspect the surface patina and workmanship. This will enable you to recognise the appearance of the genuine article. On bronze antiquities, red cuprite can form on the surface. This is extremely hard and on genuine artefacts has to be carefully scraped off using a scalpel. It can only be duplicated by using wax or paint, which is easy to remove and will reveal the fake.

Cleaning & Preserving

There are a number of cleaning kits available that come with full instructions, but like all skills it takes practice and experience to be able to clean artefacts without damaging them. In fact, there are different degrees of cleaning. Increasing the commercial value of an item in the private sector is one consideration, while extracting information about the object is another line particularly undertaken by museums or archaeologists. In general, bronze with a green patina should not be chemically cleaned. Electrolysis cleaning using washing soda or citric acid as a solution is only suitable for cleaning oxidised silver. Barrelling machines and other scouring cleaners are only suitable for use on modern items. Nothing ancient should ever be cleaned in this way as it removes the patina and softens the detail of the design. In some cases it could destroy any potential value an object might possess. Renaissance wax applied to the surface of dry or excavated bronze helps to protect the patina from chipping and moisture. It also highlights the detail by giving a slight sheen to the surface. Also remember that a collection should be stored correctly in a dry stable environment preventing objects from touching one another as bronze disease (or verdigris) can spread quickly. Isolate any item that is affected in this way and have it treated by an expert. Lead and tin objects should not be stored in a cold or damp environment as over time this causes severe deterioration (which I have witnessed on a number of occasions).

It is surprising how many artefacts or coins have been ruined by careless cleaning or poor storage. Treat all ancient items with the respect that they deserve as we are, after all, only the temporary custodians of such objects for future generations....and this applies equally to museums, archaeologists, collectors, and dealers.

Price Guide

At the end of each chapter a listing of the artefacts illustrated is given together with two values for two separate states of condition. The prices are provided as a benefit to collectors for insurance purposes and as a standard by which they can be bought or sold. The figures given are based on my own observations of dealers' prices together with recent auction results; hopefully, they represent the price a collector might expect to pay for any particular item. Because market forces constantly fluctuate, prices are subject to change both upwards and downwards. However, in the antiquity market these changes are more volatile than in other collecting fields.

In the 1980s Saxon and Viking artefacts were avidly collected by several eminent individuals. Lord McAlpine seems to have acquired almost every artefact of this period found in Britain that came onto the open market from 1985 to 1995. As a result prices rose substantially and it was very difficult to obtain pieces. Since 1995 auction results have shown a steady decline from those heady days.

An additional factor in valuing is that very few good quality antiquities found in Britain are likely to be given export licences. This means a two-tiered price system: one for the UK market and one for the global market. I believe that the global market price for previously exported items is between 50%-200% higher than the UK comparable price. Since the implementation of the Treasure Act in 1996 almost every gold or silver artefact from the Saxon and Viking era found since 1997 has been acquired by museums in the UK. This makes it almost impossible for any independent collector or foreign museum to legally acquire recent precious metal finds made in Britain. I would therefore recommend, as a long-term investment, silver and gold items that have been legally found in the past. These are likely to increase substantially in value over the next 20 years. During this time the supply of new and available material is likely to cease.

Condition

In deciding the condition of an artefact, it is the surface patina or appearance that is most critical. Just because an item is 1,000-1,500 years old does not mean that it will have a minimum value irrespective of condition. The numbers of items existing for each category of artefact have increased so that it is condition and not rarity that becomes the essential criteria. A unique item may in the future become duplicated by a recent find. This has happened consistently with coins.

Corrosion and damage will also significantly reduce the value of every artefact.

Fine (F): In this condition an artefact should be virtually complete although there may be a small piece missing. Surface patina should be stable and even but there may be slight pitting on the surface or a few minor chips around the edge. Design details should be visible but there may be wear on the high points. If there was enamel used in the original design an average of 20%-30% should remain.

A large proportion of artefacts excavated from ploughed fields are below or only just approaching Fine condition. This is due to plough damage and corrosion caused by the use of chemical fertilisers and pesticides.

Very Fine (VF): An item in this condition should be complete and have a smooth surface usually with an even patina. Design details should be sharp or clear. If enamel has been used in the design there will be an average of 60%-70% remaining. In the case of cloisonné enamelling, 75%-80% should be present.

Individual Criteria For Grading

Brooches

Very few Anglo-Saxon or Viking brooches retain their pins so this is not a factor to be considered in their grading. The majority of pagan brooches are originally from burials and these display a rust and calcite deposit on the surface. If this is covering the design then the brooch can only be classified as Fine.

Buckles

A buckle frame should be complete but the plate or pin itself may be damaged if the buckle is classified as being in Fine condition. In Very Fine the plate should be intact.

Finger Rings

In Fine condition a ring may have a slight bend in the hoop but should not be cracked. Most of the original stones should be present, although some may be chipped. In Very Fine the hoop of the ring should be unmarked. Additionally, there may be some wear on the highest points. Stones that have been recently replaced will reduce the value accordingly. It is quite common to have one or two garnets recently reset.

Iron Weapons & Knives

Due to the poor survival of most weapons I have been unable to provide a specific price structure. Swords from plough-disturbed burials are highly unstable and very difficult to treat. At present there is no easy cure. It is possible that any Anglo-Saxon iron artefact found in the ground will continue to deteriorate over a 10-year period. Only those found in anaerobic conditions (ie from rivers or lakes) are likely to be in Very Fine condition.

Dress Hooks

In Fine condition one of the stitching loops may be damaged but the hook should be present. In Very Fine condition both stitching loops plus hook should be intact.

Strap Ends

In Fine condition one of the rivet holes may be missing. The central design should be visible. In Very Fine condition all rivet holes should be intact and the design together with at least 50% of any niello inlay should be visible.

Key To Letter Coding

In order to indicate the period or origins of any particular item described in these pages a simple letter code preceding the illustration number has been used. A key to the meaning of these letter symbols is given below.

AS = Anglo-Saxon
Item manufactured by Germanic tribes in England but with a Celtic or native influence in the design. (AD 450-1066)

F = Frankish
Items manufactured on the Continent and imported into Britain by the migrating Frankish tribes, predominantly AD 410-500. The Franks were originally Teutonic people who advanced from Germany into France in the 5th century. Their influence waned by the middle of the 6th century.

M = Merovingian
Items manufactured by the Frankish dynasty that ruled Gaul during the 6th and 7th Centuries

V = Viking
(Items produced both in Scandinavia and in northern Britain between AD 793-1066 or with Scandinavian styles)

Dimensional Scales

The majority of objects illustrated in this book have been photographed alongside a CM (centimetre) scale. Most small artefacts are 150%, while larger objects are shown 100%.

Provenance

P = Find site of artefact

Acknowledgements

I would like to thank all the collectors and dealers who have allowed me to photograph and include their items especially the following:-
Richard Jewell
Norman Biggs
Mick Bott
Rob Davis
Jim Wilkinson
Alan Fordham.

I would also like to thank Mona for her encouragement and support.

Anglo-Saxon Psalter - 8th century

Chapter 1

Buckles

After the Roman Occupation of Britain the late Roman style of buckle, using zoomorphic terminals, gradually developed into new forms through the influence of migrating Germanic tribes. In the late 5th and early 6th centuries D-shaped frame buckles (see **F1**) came into use. This example is in bronze, and has a D-shaped buckle frame with animal heads at either end. There is a ring and dot pattern around the outer edge of the frame, which is stepped. The buckle plate is square shaped, hinged and has three rivets. The plate is decorated with an engraved design of two fishes within a border of straight lines and grooves. This is influenced by Byzantine art. The tongue (pin) extends over the top of the frame of the buckle. The likely dating of this piece is late 5th century.

Another buckle with a rectangular plate and D-shaped loop is shown as **F2**. The design consists of a series of dots forming two crosses on the plate. At the base of this is an extended trefoil, which contains two rivet holes that appear to form the eyes of two birds. This example again dates from the late 5th century.

F2
Late 5th century bronze buckle, decorated plate.

F1
Bronze buckle, 5th century, decorated plate.

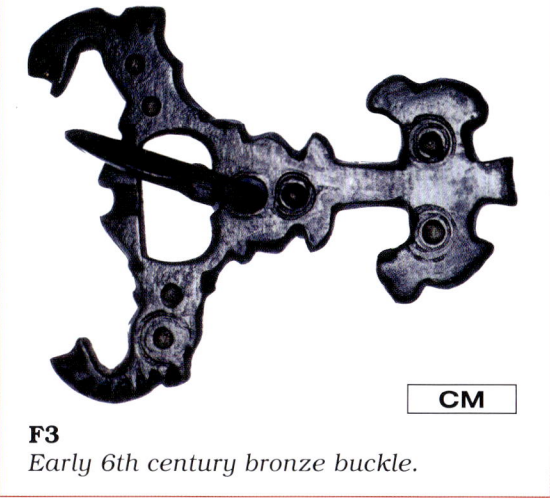

F3
Early 6th century bronze buckle.

Another Germanic buckle is shown as **F3**. This has zoomorphic terminals extending outwards from the buckle frame. Cast in one piece, with a ring and dot decoration, this buckle resembles a scorpion in its overall appearance. It is likely to date to the early 6th century.

One distinctive form of buckle tongue has Frankish origins (from the Rhineland). It is referred to as shield-shaped or sometimes violin-shaped. A simple example is shown in **F4**. This has a shield-shaped tongue inset with a garnet beneath which it has a gold foil backing. This dates between AD 525-625. As it was found in England, it is likely to fall late within this date range.

F4
Shield shaped buckle tongue.

CM

During the Anglo-Saxon period belt buckles were worn mainly by women. This has been established from the discovery of buckles in position around the waist in female graves dating from the 6th and early 7th centuries. Small circular iron buckles have been found in male graves, but appear to have been used on straps for supporting the shield. However, it is common to find two small oval buckles in graves, their position indicating that they were used to fasten a knife sheath to a waist belt.

Buckles were principally made of bronze or iron, but examples have also been found made of bone with bronze or iron tongues.

The small example of a bronze buckle, **AS5**, was cast in one piece, and has an oval loop and triangular plate. It may have been used to fasten a knife sheath to a waist belt as described above. It is likely to date from the 6th century.

Another buckle of Frankish origin is shown as **F6**. This is bronze with a D-shaped loop, and the tongue is extended considerably past the end of the loop. The plate is separately cast and hinged to the loop and tongue; in this example it has been damaged. Buckles with a flattened, rectangular frame date from the late 5th to early 6th century.

AS5
6th century small bronze buckle.

CM

F6
Late 5th century bronze buckle.

CM

In Kent during the 6th and early 7th centuries oval buckles were fixed to a distinctive form of plate, which was triangular with three rivets. **AS7** is a bronze example with an oval loop decorated with transverse lines (a distinctive feature of Anglo-Saxon buckles). The rivets (one of which is missing) have large domed bosses. There is also additional decoration on the plate of ring and dot pattern. This buckle dates late 6th century.

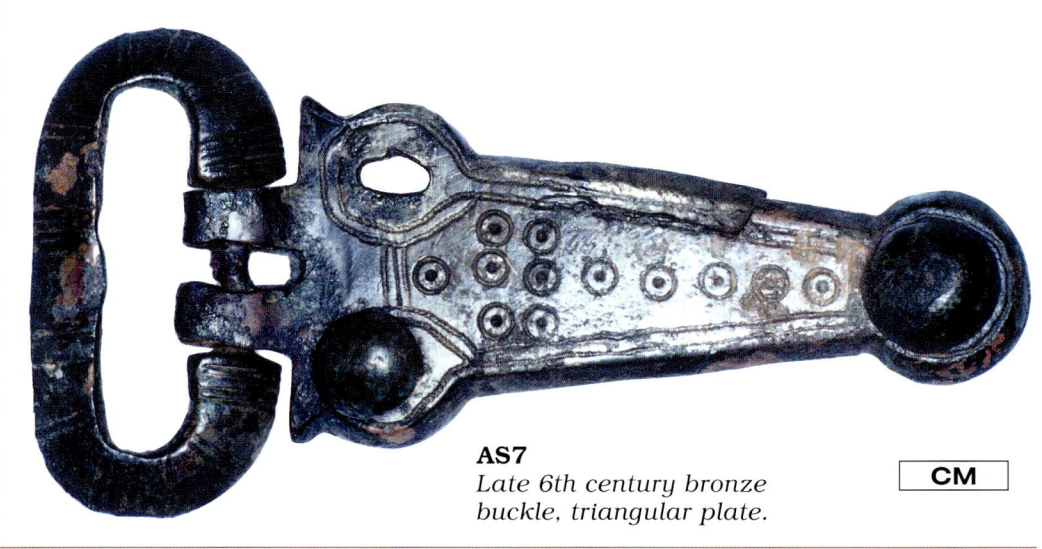

AS7
Late 6th century bronze buckle, triangular plate.

CM

Another example of this type of buckle is shown as **AS8**. This example is smaller with a tinned bronze surface and is cast in one piece. The buckle tongue may have been iron as there is rust residue on the hinge. Gold examples of the Kentish type exist, set with garnets and lapis lazuli, and with filigree decoration on the plate. These are 7th century in date.

AS8 *Small tinned bronze buckle.*

Large ornate buckles are also known on the Continent as reliquaries. They would have formed part of a belt-shaped shrine, which was believed to have bestowed healing on the wearer. These date from the 7th and 8th centuries.

In the 7th century bronze buckles, cast in one piece and with cut out decoration on the plate, were produced as cheaper copies of the garnet inlaid examples worn by the wealthy. The elaborate plates used on such buckles are normally square or rectangular in shape with a centrally mounted garnet. The surrounding field is of chip-carved design. This is usually with a zoomorphic theme of Style I, and would date mid 6th century.

AS9
Late 6th century small bronze buckle.

A small solid bronze D-shaped buckle is shown as **AS9**. This has an expanded hoop with transverse grooves giving it a scalloped form. It is likely to be 6th or 7th century in date.

It is very difficult to accurately date Anglo-Saxon buckles from the late 7th to early 9th century. This is because the practice of pagan burial had ceased due to the dominance of Christianity; subsequently buckles (and other personal belongings) were no longer interred in graves.

AS10
Mid 9th century bronze buckle with silver panel.
P - *Cambridgeshire*

The beautiful bronze buckle shown as **AS10** was cast in two pieces. It has a pointed D-shaped decorated loop. The plate is waisted and inset with a repousse stamped silver foil panel. This is decorated with an interlaced ribbon pattern, which gives it a date of mid 9th century. There are two rivet holes at the bottom of the plate and the tongue has a zoomorphic terminal.

During the 9th to 11th centuries buckles made of iron were usually D-shaped. These are often part of horse furniture.

AS11
Small gilt bronze buckle, late 6th century. **P** - *Kent*

A series of buckles with oval or circular frames have an integrally cast zoomorphic head at one end forming the buckle plate. **AS11** is of fine style. It is of gilded bronze with an iron tongue. There is a circular stud underneath the plate for attachment to the belt. The head or facemask has circular eyes with a raised brow and braided hair with a central parting. It may date from the late 6th century.

AS12
Bronze zoomorphic buckle, 9th century.
P - *Lincolnshire*

Another example also in bronze is **AS12**. This is of more elongated form with an oval loop and bronze tongue. There is a zoomorphic terminal at the lower end with raised circular eyes and an extended snout with the ears forming part of the buckle loop. The buckle plate comprises a facemask with simple features and three holes at the top that contained the rivets for connecting the buckle to the belt. This buckle possibly dates to the 9th century.

A more elaborate bronze buckle is shown as **V14** which would date from the late 10th to the early 11th century. It has two biting beasts gripping the crossbar and there is also a crest at the apex, which again represents a knot. However, the stylistic form is very abstract and suggests an influence of both Jellinge and Ringerike styles. The integrally cast plate is decorated with an overlapping series of chiselled-out lines. This is a characteristic feature of 11th century Viking art.

V13
11th century Ringerike style buckle.

V15
11th century Urnes style buckle. **P** - *Suffolk*

During the Viking period buckles became more ornamental with stylised designs representing Viking art. **V13** has a D-shaped loop in copper alloy incorporating very crude Ringerike style decoration, which dates it to the 11th century. At the apex of the buckle is a crest representing a knot with ribbon like strands coming from each side and ending in a coil. Two biting beasts grip the crossbar.

The tongue appears to have been made of iron and there are two iron rivets at the widest end of the plate.

A most beautiful Viking buckle is **V15** which is copper alloy and dates from the mid 11th century. It is in the Urnes style with the projecting animal's head forming the tongue of the buckle. This is integrally cast with the buckle plate. The latter is hinged onto the crossbar of the buckle, which has two biting beasts with lentoid eyes supporting it. The bodies are ribbon like with curving lines intertwining around them. It is of openwork form, which is a typical feature of Urnes style. This buckle was found in Suffolk.

V14
Late 10th century bronze buckle, decorated.

Another late Viking buckle is shown as **V16** which is bronze with a D-shaped loop. There are two biting beasts gripping the crossbar as usual, but the design around the hoop is very abstract and in quite high relief. The ribbon-like bodies are still interlacing but the overall form of the buckle is approaching the Romanesque style of art of the 12th century.

V16
Late 11th century decorated bronze buckle.

Price Guide

		Fine	Very Fine			Fine	Very Fine
F1	Bronze buckle, 5th century, decorated plate.	£75	£190	**AS9**	Late 6th century small bronze buckle.	£6	£15
F2	Late 5th century bronze buckle, decorated plate.	£50	£130	**AS10**	Late 9th century bronze buckle with silver panel.	£120	£300
F3	Early 6th century bronze buckle.	£50	£125	**AS11**	Small gilt bronze buckle, late 6th century.	£30	£75
F4	Shield shaped buckle tongue.	£9	£18	**AS12**	Bronze zoomorphic buckle, 8th century.	£28	£70
AS5	6th century small bronze buckle.	£18	£45	**V13**	11th century Ringerike style buckle.	£26	£65
F6	Late 5th century bronze buckle.	£12	£28	**V14**	Late 10th century bronze buckle, decorated.	£70	£180
AS7	Late 6th century bronze buckle, triangular plate.	£85	£220	**V15**	11th century Urnes style buckle.	£275	£800
AS8	Small tinned bronze buckle.	£24	£65	**V16**	Late 11th century decorated bronze buckle.	£40	£120

Chapter 2

Strap Ends

During the Roman period in Britain metal reinforced belts were used by the military and this continued, albeit to a much lesser degree, after the Roman army had left. The decorations used included metal strap ends, which were fixed to the end of the belt as a form of protection and to act as a weighted terminal. Strap ends were multi-purpose in function, used primarily in pairs, and we believe them to have been fitted principally to sword belts and horse harness straps. They were most popular in the Anglo-Saxon period during the 8th-10th centuries AD, when they became highly decorative and stylised. Before this time the use of strap ends was far more rare and such examples that did exist were fairly plain in style.

An example of an early strap end in silver is **MV21**. This is likely to have been imported from the Continent during the late 6th century AD. It is rectangular in form and has a rounded end. The design has been chip carved with segmented grooves and the surface has been gilded. There are two rivets at the split end, which received the belt. The back is plain.

MV21 Silver gilt strap end. P - Kent CM

The dating of strap ends is based primarily on two important hoards that were found in Britain. The first is the Cuerdale Hoard, found in Lancashire in 1840. It was buried by the Vikings around AD 905. It included coins and hack silver, and weighed in total 40 kilos. Many of the artefacts in the hoard have a central cruciform design. The second important discovery is the Trewhiddle Hoard, found in Cornwall in 1774. This has been dated from the coins included in it to around AD 870. Within this distinctive silver hoard were a series of strap ends and fittings featuring animal designs of a style now named after this hoard.

In addition to the two hoards mentioned above, individual discoveries of strap ends have been made by both archaeologists and metal detectorists. The quantity found over the last 25 years, in fact, has been phenomenal; these mainly represent detector finds recovered from ploughed fields. Because of this increase in known examples, a better understanding of the development of styles has resulted. However, a close dating of strap ends is still difficult unless they are found in conjunction with coins.

During the late 8th and early 9th centuries strap ends took on a much more decorative and stylised form. Strap ends from this period were made with double rivets at the split end, and a plain back. They have a central design showing quadrupeds entwined in foliage. In addition, there is usually a stylised palmette or scroll design on the split end between the rivets. The animal head terminal has a wedge shaped decoration between the ears, which are usually scrolled.

AS22
Bronze strap end
with panel of three beasts. CM

AS22 is an example in bronze with an animal head terminal that is evident when the strap end is looked at from above. This has comma shaped or scrolled ears, which are a feature found principally in the north of Britain. Round-shaped ears are a southern feature. The centre decorative panel has three beasts set against a niello background. All of these beasts have speckled bodies.

AS23 is a slightly later example. The animal head terminal has rounded ears, and the eyes have been drilled out to receive glass insets (now missing). The nose is shortened with a flattened end. The field has a quadruped with its head turned back. The sides of the strap end are beaded.

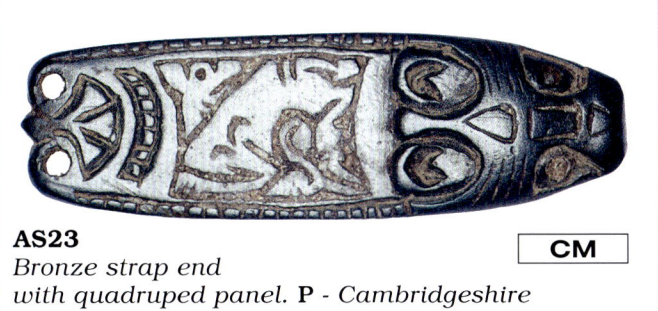

AS23
*Bronze strap end
with quadruped panel.* **P** - *Cambridgeshire*   CM

Strap ends during the 9th century were often produced in silver and these are usually of better quality and more decorative than their bronze counterparts. **AS24** is a silver example with the field design composed of four quadrupeds set around a lozenge shaped central panel. The design has been filled

AS24
Silver strap end, panel with four quadrupeds.   CM

with niello inlay, which due to blistering can make it difficult to clearly see the shape of the beasts. The animal head terminal has rounded ears with an oval ornamentation between. The nostrils are inlaid with niello and the raised eyes would have received glass inlay.

A further example in silver (**AS25**) shows cruder or more abstract imagery. There are two circular panels each containing four compartments set around a central lozenge. The animals have degenerated into geometric lines

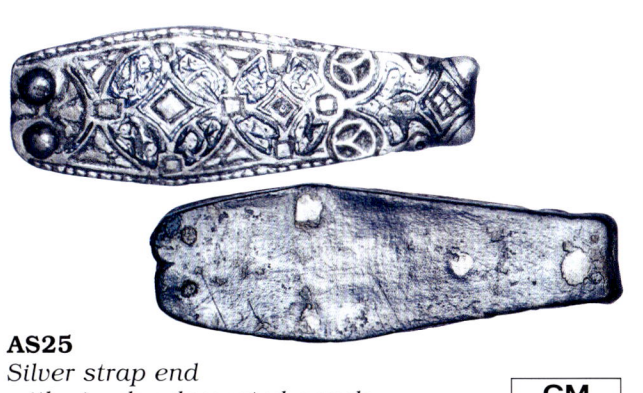

AS25
*Silver strap end
with circular decorated panels.*   CM

outlined with niello. The animal head terminal now has circular ears divided into three segments. The eyes are circular and quite small with a niello panel in between; the snout is shortened and flattened. The sides of the strap end are curving and beaded. The split end still has two silver rivets intact. On the reverse the surface is plain but there are four flattened rivets attaching the back plate to the front.

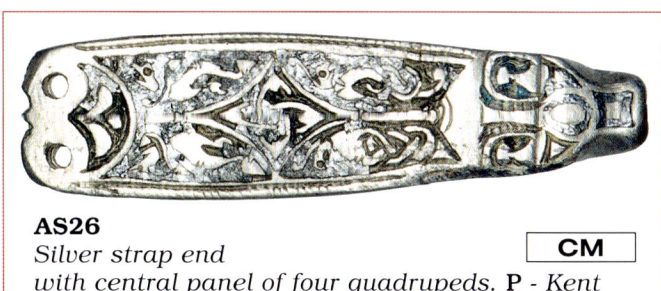

AS26
*Silver strap end
with central panel of four quadrupeds.* **P** - *Kent*   CM

AS26 is another variety from the late 9th century, again of silver. It has four quadrupeds that are all outlined with niello inlay, and each is set in one corner of a cross. The central lozenge panel has an interlaced design. The animal head terminal has oval ears while the eyes are triangular. These features are again all outlined in niello inlay.

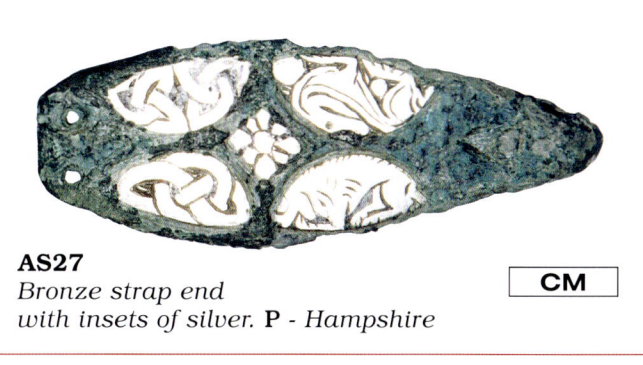

AS27
*Bronze strap end
with insets of silver.* **P** - *Hampshire*   CM

Many strap ends from the 9th century use silver panels set on to a bronze backing plate. **AS27** has five individually designed insets of silver. The bottom two are of quadrupeds, while the top two have an interlaced ribbon pattern. In the centre is a lozenge shaped floral motif. The animal head terminal is very crude and has corroded so it is difficult to determine its features.

AS28 is a silver strap end, of late 9th century date, with fairly crude features. The central panel is square, with an abstract design, and is inlaid with enamel. The sides are beaded and the animal head terminal has a lozenge panel decorated with a cross.

AS28
*Silver strap end
abstract design.* **P** - *S Yorkshire*

Enlargement

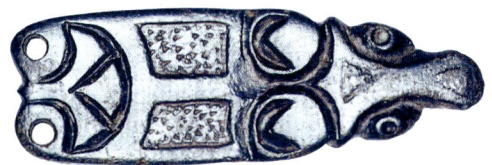

AS31
*Bronze strap end,
missing inset panels.* **P** - *S Cambridgeshire*

Strap ends dating from the 9th century were often locally produced. A fragment of a mould for a strap end was found at Carlisle, which indicates a workshop in that area.

One important factor is the use of silver wire in the central panel. **AS29** is an example of this. Made of bronze, it has a central panel with an "S" scroll punctuated by horseshoe shapes. These are of silver wire set into a niello field. The example illustrated has an additional silver

A smaller example of this type of strap end (**AS31**) has two small rectangular panels that have been notched to receive the niello and wire inlay. This has now fallen out. The animal's head has round ears with drilled out eyes and extended snout. There are two rivet holes between which there is a trilobate leaf design.

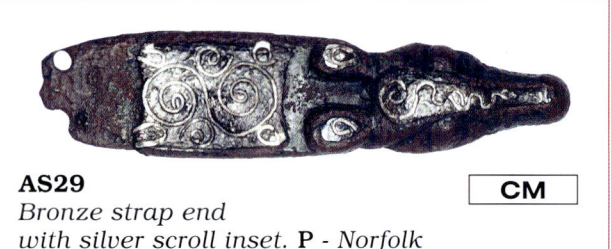

AS29
*Bronze strap end
with silver scroll inset.* **P** - *Norfolk*

AS32
*Bronze strap end
with silver scroll work.* **P** - *Suffolk*

scroll set into the ears, and also on the panel between the eyes and along the snout. This type of strap end is commonly found in East Anglia, Norfolk and Suffolk being the principal counties. Sometimes the silver wire scrolls are set in an enamel field rather than niello, but this is quite rare. The "S" scroll strap end is quite prolific and I have encountered numerous examples, usually 3-6cm in length.

Another example of "S" scroll work is shown as **AS32**. This is late 9th century in date, and has a single rectangular panel of silver wire set into a niello field. The animal head terminal has oval ears, formed by a circular and a crescent shaped punch. The eyes are raised beads, and there is a lozenge shaped panel of silver wire on the forehead.

AS33
*Bronze strap end with
silver scroll design and animal head terminals.*

AS30
*Bronze strap end
with two panels of scrolled design.*

The second variety, which is illustrated as **AS30** has two rectangular panels. Again it has silver wire of "S" scroll form inlaid into niello. The animal head terminal has extended oval ears, lozenge shaped eyes, and a pronounced snout. There is a small area of silver wire on the forehead.

Another example shown as **AS33** and again of East Anglian manufacture, probably dates to the beginning of the 10th century. It has a central rectangular panel of three pairs of silver scrolls, but there is an animal head terminal at both ends. The split end has a single rivet hole through the nostril. The ears are oval in shape and there is an additional silver panel, between the eyes, which has been drilled to receive glass

AS34
Bronze strap end quadruped central panel.

AS37
Elongated bronze strap end herringbone design.

insets. The absence of a leaf motif, together with the duplication of the animal head, suggests a later date for this type of strap end.

A bronze strap end, which incorporates a quadruped and also an interlaced ribbon design, is shown as **AS34**. This is a feature more commonly found in the north of England with a suggested longevity of use. The animal head terminal has round ears, and there are two comma shaped forms between the ears.

Another example, **AS37**, again of bronze, is also of elongated form with straight sides. This example has a rounded animal head terminal with a central panel composed of crude lines referred to as "herringbone" design. For this example, I would suggest a late 9th or even an early 10th century date.

V38
Bronze strap end, three animal heads.

AS35
Bronze strap end with floral decoration. **P** - *Suffolk*

The gradual deterioration from an animal design (typified by the Trewhiddle Hoard) into a geometric pattern occurred during the late 9th and early 10th centuries.

AS35 is bronze, with a central panel of four ovals each containing an interlaced design. This suggests a slightly later 9th century date when floral decoration - and then simple lines - replaced zoomorphic decorations.

AS.36. is a bronze strap end of thin elongated form with crude and simple detailing. The central rectangular panel is composed of a lozenge with triangular shapes around this in a slightly haphazard form. The animal head terminal has a square end, with simple curves indicating the eyes. Again, this is probably of late 9th century date.

One series incorporates several animal heads repeated down the length of the strap end. An example of this is **V38**. Here there are three animal heads. Two face downwards, while the central head is reversed and facing backwards. Most of these strap ends come from the north of Britain (especially Yorkshire), and they appear to derive from a Scandinavian form. The butt end is now a single piece of metal flattened out and has two rivet holes or sometimes only one. This flattened form of butt end appears to be a predominantly 10th century characteristic, and is also a typically Viking design.

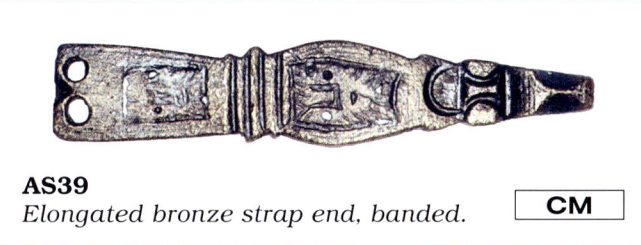

AS39
Elongated bronze strap end, banded.

AS36
Elongated bronze strap end, simple design. **P** - *Berkshire*

An example, found in the River Thames (**AS39**) - again of elongated form - is unusual in having four bands in the centre of the strap end, which act as a division for the two central panels. Each of these displays a very crude animal design and shows traces of enamel niello inlay. The animal head terminal has semi-

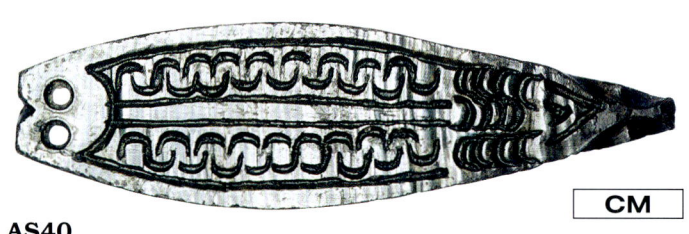

AS40
Bronze strap end, simple crescent design. **P** - *Durham*

V43 is an openwork example with a fantastic animal evident when the strap end is viewed from above. The central body has two pellets representing eyes and a pair of wings indicated by grooves. This could represent a dragon or even a bird. The two rivets are set into a recessed panel and this indicates a late 10th century or early 11th century date.

circular grooves forming the ears. This example is again probably early 10th century in date.

Another late example of a strap end, probably 10th century, is **AS40**. The sides are curved, and it has a simple narrow animal head terminal. The central decoration is composed of a series of interlocking crescents in two bands divided by two parallel lines.

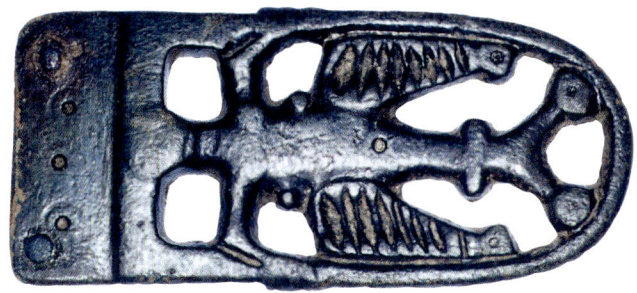

V43
Viking openwork bronze strap end, winged creature. **P** - *Cambridgeshire*

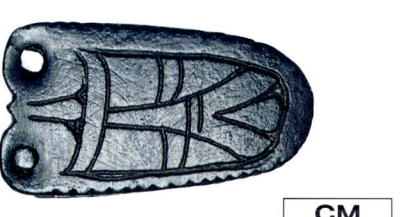

V41
Tongue-shaped bronze strap end, Ringerike design.

During the 10th and 11th century strap ends became broader and tongue-shaped. **V41** is a small example with a rounded terminal now devoid of an animal's head. The central design is very simple and takes the form of curving lines in the Ringerike Style. There is a scallop edge, which is unusual for this period.

Further examples of tongue-shaped strap ends are **V44** and **AS45**. The design on these may represent a tree, indicated in two different styles. The first is very simplistic, while the latter is more intricate with animals and birds positioned around the icanthus follage motifs. This is late 10th

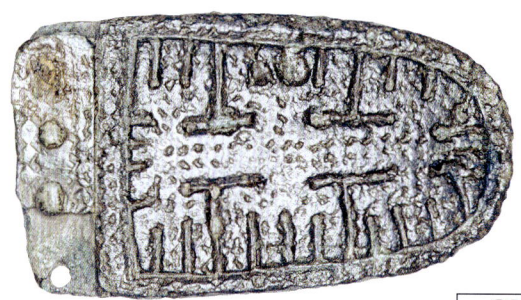

V44
Viking tongue shaped bronze strap end. **P** - *Durham*

V42
Viking strap end, tongue shaped, Borre style.

Another Viking strap end is shown as **V42**. This has a ring and dot pattern at the butt end, with an interlaced design covering the rest of the strap end in the Borre style. It would date from the 10th century.

Many of the strap ends of this period are quite intricately ornamented, and carry an abstract design that can display strong Viking features.

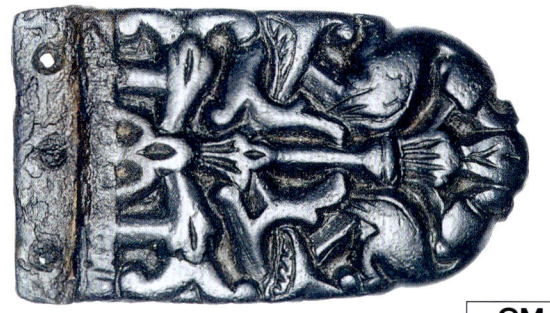

AS45
Tongue shaped bronze strap end. **P** - *Suffolk*

century in date from the Winchester style.

The final development of the strap end (see **AS46**) came about in the 11th and early 12th centuries when the animal head terminal became three-dimensional with circular indented eyes, triangular raised ears, and a flat tapering body expanding out at the split butt end. There is a simple double lozenge pattern in the centre, ring and dot motifs on the terminal, and beaded borders. This form of animal head terminal continued in use into the 13th and 14th centuries.

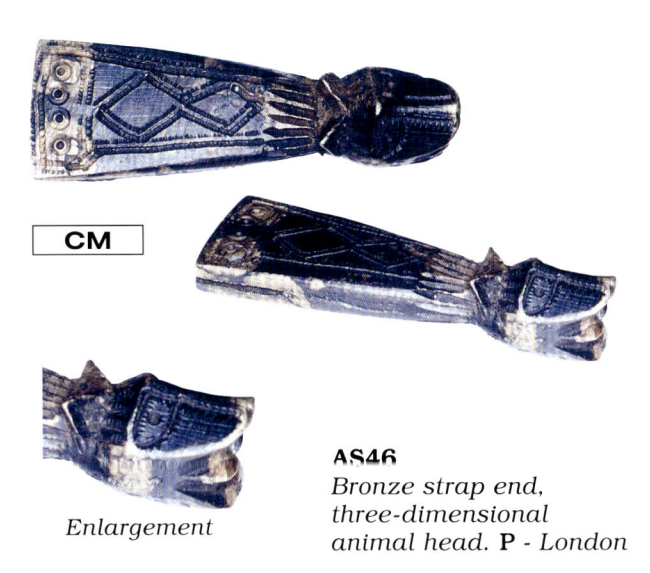

Enlargement

AS46
Bronze strap end, three-dimensional animal head. **P** - *London*

Price Guide

		Fine	Very Fine			Fine	Very Fine
MV21	Silver gilt strap end.	£140	£325	**AS34**	Bronze strap end quadruped central panel.	£65	£160
AS22	Bronze strap end with panel of three beasts.	£160	£400	**AS35**	Bronze strap end with floral decoration.	£60	£145
AS23	Bronze strap end with quadruped panel.	£70	£180	**AS36**	Elongated bronze strap end, simple design.	£40	£100
AS24	Silver strap end, panel with four quadrupeds.	£450	£1,100	**AS37**	Elongated bronze strap end herringbone design.	£35	£85
AS25	Silver strap end with circular decorated panels.	£500	£1,200	**V38**	Bronze strap end, three animal heads.	£45	£120
AS26	Silver strap end with central panel of four quadrupeds.	£550	£1,300	**AS39**	Elongated bronze strap end, banded.	£50	£140
AS27	Bronze strap end with insets of silver.	£175	£450	**AS40**	Bronze strap end, simple crescent design.	£30	£75
AS28	Silver strap end abstract design.	£275	£650	**V41**	Tongue-shaped bronze strap end, simple design.	£25	£65
AS29	Bronze strap end with silver scroll inset.	£140	£375	**V42**	Viking strap end, tongue shaped, abstract design.	£70	£200
AS30	Bronze strap end with two panels of scrolled design.	£110	£300	**V43**	Viking openwork bronze strap end, winged creature.	£75	£230
AS31	Bronze strap end, missing inset panels.	£30	£70	**V44**	Viking tongue shaped bronze strap end.	£55	£150
AS32	Bronze strap end with silver scroll work.	£90	£250	**AS45**	Tongue shaped bronze strap end.	£80	£250
AS33	Bronze strap end with silver scroll design and animal head terminals.	£130	£350	**AS46**	Bronze strap end, three-dimensional animal head.	£50	£140

Cruciform Brooch

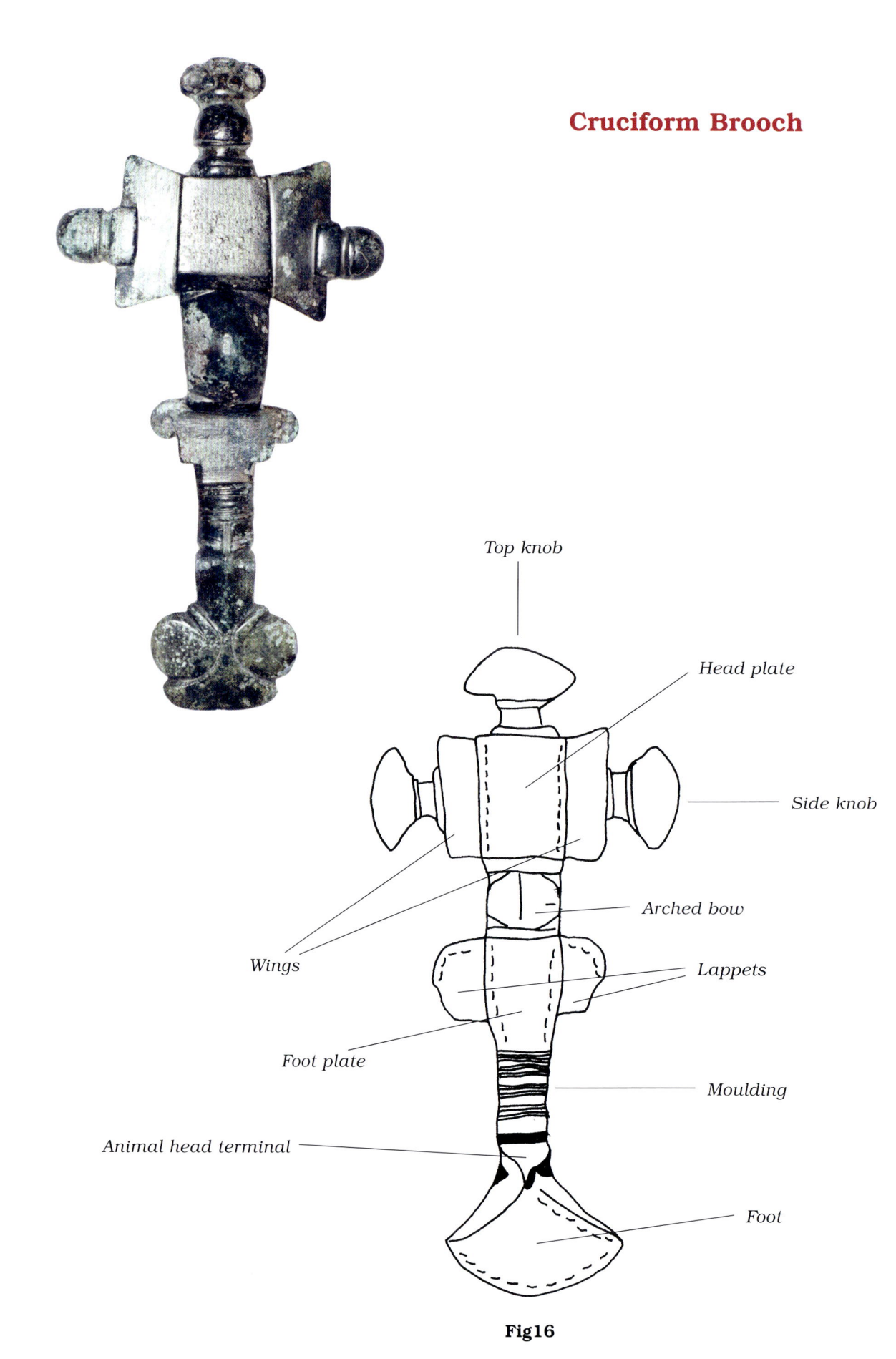

Fig 16

Chapter 3
Cruciform, Long & Equal-Arm Brooches

During the 5th century the late Roman crossbow fibula was adapted by the Saxons into a new style representing the final development of the fibula brooch. This was the cruciform, square-headed and radiate-headed style brooches. From the large number that have been excavated from pagan burials it has been possible to provide a sequence of dating starting with quite simple forms of cruciform brooch in the 5th and 6th centuries, and developing into the richly ornamented types of the later 6th and early 7th centuries.

AS47 is an early example of a bronze cruciform brooch dating from the mid 5th century. It has a very small head plate with an integral rounded head knob. The high arched bow is the same width as the head plate. The extended narrow foot has a zoomorphic terminal. This brooch, as with so many others of this type, is missing the side knobs, which would have formed the cross (hence the name of the brooch). These were attached by means of an iron axis bar on the early examples, but on this example the bar has corroded away. Sometimes the side knobs were soldered onto the head plate for extra strength but this is a later occurrence. In the side view photograph it is possible to see the extended catch plate, which is also tapered to receive the iron pin. This feature was a continuation of the crossbow brooch, and was replaced during the late 5th century by a much shorter catch plate.

Most cruciform brooches were worn individually by women on the breast (the most common position they are found on the body in burials). Additionally, a pair of smaller bronze brooches were often worn at the shoulders.

A much more developed example of a cruciform brooch is **AS48**. The head plate is rectangular with expanded wings and the top and side knobs have been integrally cast with the brooch. These are rounded in form with simple collars. There is a row of annulet punches down the sides of the head plate. The bow has a high arch but is much shorter than that of the previous example. There is a zoomorphic terminal on the foot

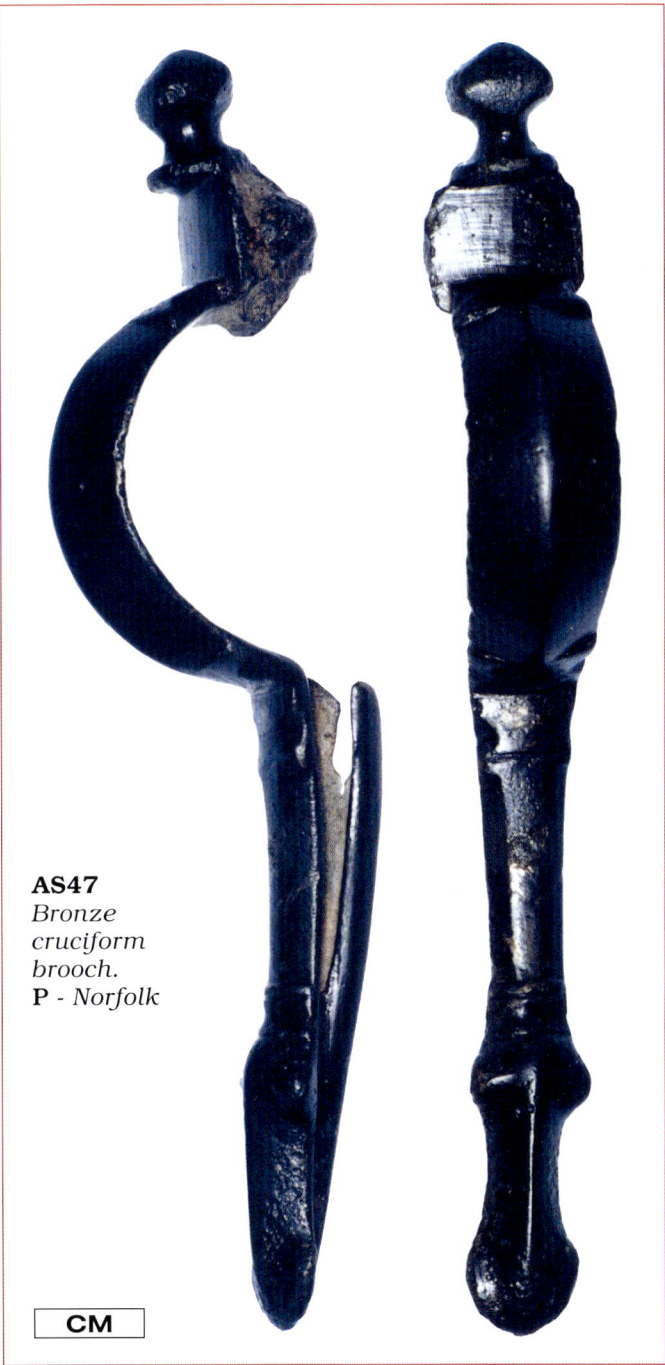

AS47
Bronze cruciform brooch.
P - *Norfolk*

CM

with prominent circular eyes. The nostrils are circular and flaring. There is a crescent shaped foot terminal, with a line of annulets running down the centre. This example is typically East Anglian in style and would date circa AD 500.

A slightly later example, probably dating from the early 6th century is **AS49**. It has a trapezoid-shaped head plate with rectangular wings rounded at the corners. The head knob and side knobs are again integrally cast with the brooch and are rounded in form. The arched bow has faceted corners and is concave on the underside. This brooch has additional rectangular lappets, one on each side, attached to the trapezoid field between the bow and the foot. Each of the lappets is finely moulded with a pair of eyes and eyebrows. The zoomorphic foot has very simple bulbous mouldings for the eyes and small oval nostrils.

Another bronze cruciform brooch shown as **AS50** dates from the early to mid 6th century. It again has a trapezoid head plate with expanding wings, rounded side knobs and an enlarged head knob. This feature is unusual as it has a facemask extending from it. This has a moulded

AS50
Large bronze cruciform brooch zoomorphic terminal.

CM

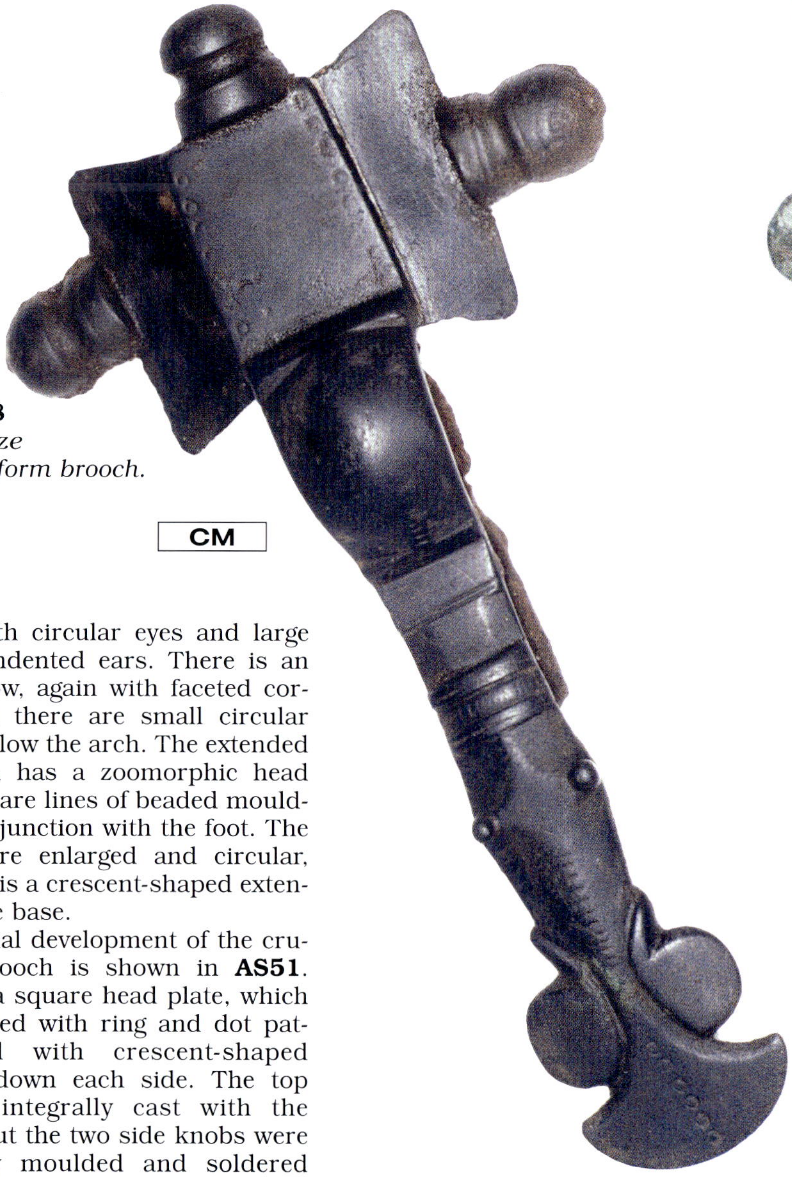

AS48
Bronze cruciform brooch.

CM

design with circular eyes and large circular indented ears. There is an arched bow, again with faceted corners, and there are small circular lappets below the arch. The extended foot again has a zoomorphic head and there are lines of beaded moulding at the junction with the foot. The nostrils are enlarged and circular, and there is a crescent-shaped extension at the base.

The final development of the cruciform brooch is shown in **AS51**. This has a square head plate, which is decorated with ring and dot pattern and with crescent-shaped punches down each side. The top knob is integrally cast with the brooch, but the two side knobs were separately moulded and soldered onto the sides of the head plate. The

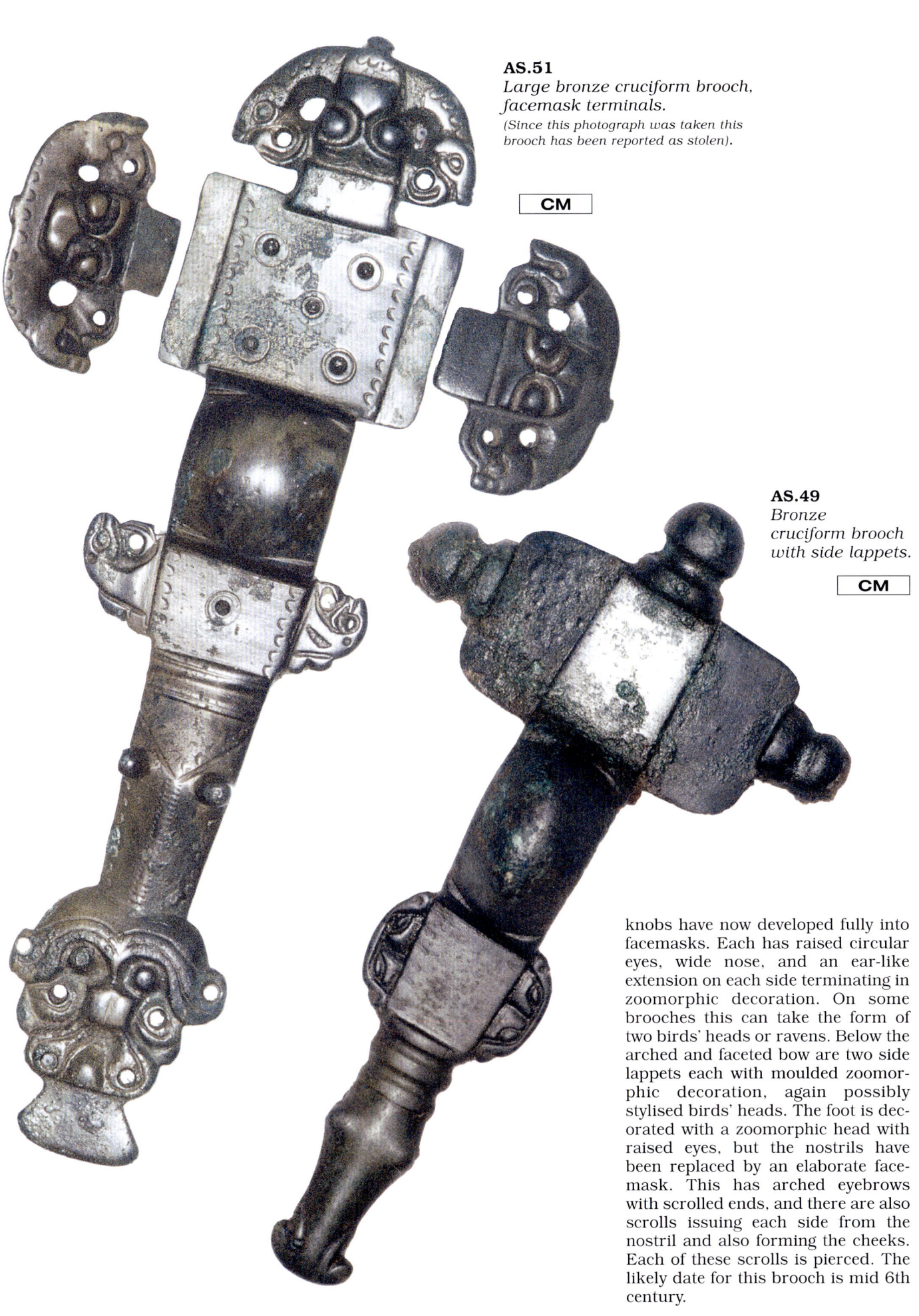

AS.51
Large bronze cruciform brooch, facemask terminals.
(Since this photograph was taken this brooch has been reported as stolen).

CM

AS.49
Bronze cruciform brooch with side lappets.

CM

knobs have now developed fully into facemasks. Each has raised circular eyes, wide nose, and an ear-like extension on each side terminating in zoomorphic decoration. On some brooches this can take the form of two birds' heads or ravens. Below the arched and faceted bow are two side lappets each with moulded zoomorphic decoration, again possibly stylised birds' heads. The foot is decorated with a zoomorphic head with raised eyes, but the nostrils have been replaced by an elaborate facemask. This has arched eyebrows with scrolled ends, and there are also scrolls issuing each side from the nostril and also forming the cheeks. Each of these scrolls is pierced. The likely date for this brooch is mid 6th century.

AS52
Small bronze long brooch.

AS53
Small bronze long brooch with side lappets.

A smaller form of Anglo-Saxon fibula brooch is referred to as a small long brooch. These were normally worn in pairs at the shoulder. They originated early in the 5th century and their use continued well into the 6th century. **AS52** is an early example with a square head, which has a decoration around the sides consisting of punched dots. There is an arched ridged bow and the foot is triangular in outline with bevelled sides and a flattened discoid terminal.

A slightly latter example **AS53** has a trapezoid head plate with rounded lobes on the upper corners. In the centre of the head plate there is a raised rectangular field. There are circular punches on the top edge and trefoil motifs with a circular terminal down the sides. The arched bow is ridged with faceted corners and the foot expands into a triangular terminal. There are two square lappets set just below the bow with punched dots down the sides. There is also a raised moulding with three transverse bands in the middle section of the footplate. This example is early 6th century in date and is typically East Anglian in form.

A number of small long brooches developed cruciform head plates. **AS54** is an example in bronze with a rectangular head plate, which is notched each side of the bow and on the upper corners. There is also a circular perforation in the upper corners. Triangular punches run along the top and side edges. The arched bow is ridged in the centre with faceted corners, and is concave on the underside. The foot has a flattened T-shaped terminal with triangular punch marks around the edges. This brooch is again early 6th century in date.

Probably the most commonly encountered form of all the long brooches is **AS55**. This has the head plate forming a trefoil with a central square. The arched bow is again ridged with faceted corners. The footplate has bevelled sides and is moulded with transverse bands in the middle. There is a triangular terminal with a thickened ridge at the bottom, which is decorated with moulded lines. This would again date early 6th century.

An unusual variant of this brooch is **AS56**, which has a ridged arched bow with a trapezoid head plate at

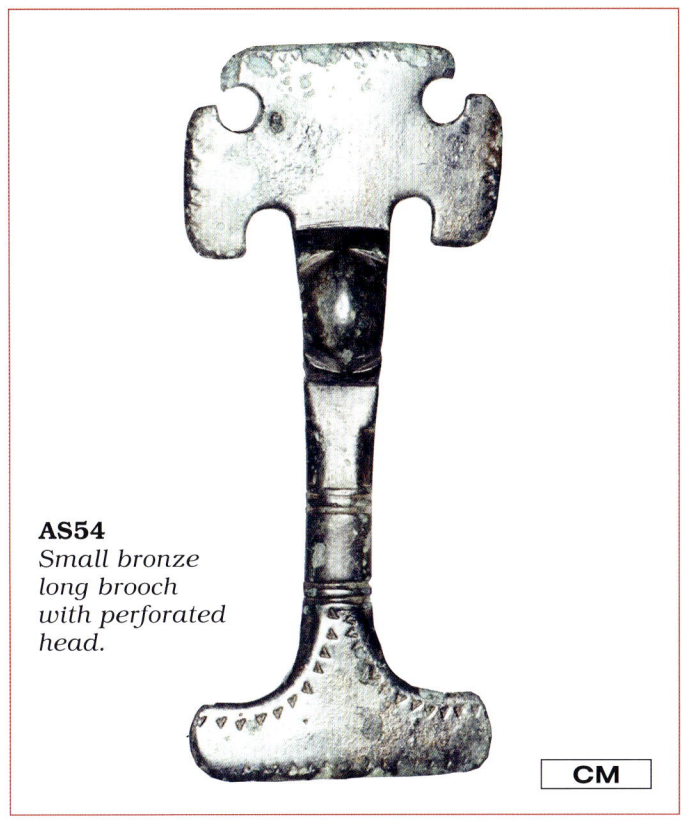

AS54
Small bronze long brooch with perforated head.

AS55
Small bronze long brooch, trefoil head.

each end with trefoil terminals. This is called an equal-armed brooch and it is more commonly found on Continental sites, especially in Germany and Scandinavia. It dates to the early 6th century and is characteristically East Anglian in style.

Another type of small fibula brooch is referred to as a small square headed type. These are quite often gilded as in **AS57**. This example has raised rectangular moulding on the head plate with a chip carved design. There is a very short, gently arched bow, which is flattened in form with a central ridge. The chip carved design on each side continues from the head plate as vertical lines down to the shoulders of the footplate ending in zoomorphic heads. These have round eyes and an extended mouth. The footplate has a cruciform design of a cross with a central boss. This type of brooch originates from Kent and dates from the early to mid 6th century. During this period their use extended throughout southern Britain.

AS56
Bronze Equal armed brooch, trefoil ends.

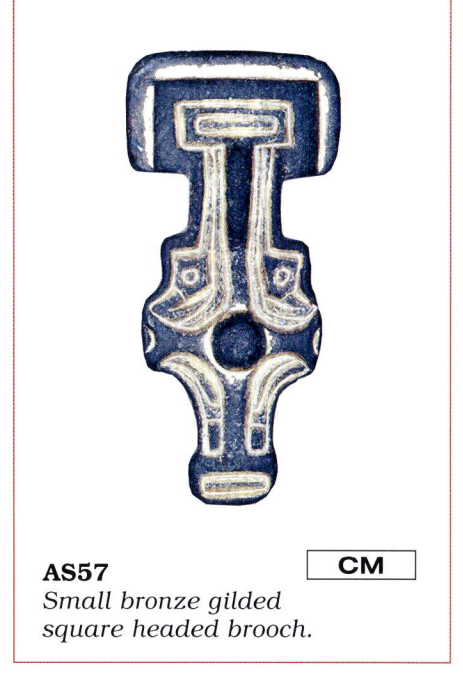

AS57
Small bronze gilded square headed brooch.

A larger square headed brooch is shown as **AS58**. This is gilt bronze with an ornate chip-carved design. It can also be classified as a cruciform brooch. It has a rectangular head plate with extensions at the lower sides. The border is decorated with facemasks on each side. There is an arched bow, which is ridged with faceted corners. Below the arch is a trapezoidal field with perforated lappets on each side. These are decorated with a bird-like design. The foot is ovoid, has a facemask with round eyes, a scrolled moustache, and wedge shaped mouth. The terminal is crescent shaped. This example is early to mid 6th century in date.

The most decorative of all of the Anglo-Saxon brooches are the large square headed types. **AS59** is a good example. It represents more of a symbol of status than a functional brooch. The fact that most surviving examples come from pagan burials, could suggest that they were made specifically as grave goods. They originate in Scandinavia during the 5th century. In Norway, for example, they have been dated to as early as AD 400. However, they were introduced to England in the late 5th century and continued in use to around AD 575. As can be seen from the photograph, almost every area of the brooch has been decorated and heavily gilded. Occasionally, garnets or glass inlay are used.

AS59 has a rectangular head plate with a central inverted facemask with circular eyes, arched brow and a semi-circular nose. On each side is a curvilinear swastika contained within a rectangular field. At the top of the head plate is a chip-carved zoomorphic design while on each side are a row of horizontal billets. These are separated from the central design by a raised rectangular ridge with oval projections at the top. The short arched bow has a prominent centre rib with a circular boss and a chip carved zoomorphic design on either side. The footplate has a lozenge shaped field with zoomorphic facemasks at the corners. There are splayed side lobes and a terminal lobe. This has a large facemask with circular eyes, a scrolled end moustache, and a mouth in the form of a C-scroll. Brooches of this type date c520-550.

Another example, **AS60** is slightly smaller but is decorated in a similar style. The rectangular head plate has a small central facemask with square panels on each side. There is a strand of cable moulding just above this. In the outer field

AS58
Gilt bronze square headed brooch with side lappets.

CM

there is a zoomorphic chip carved decoration. The bow again has a prominent rib with a circular boss and chip carving on the sides. The footplate has a lozenge shaped field with a central boss, and again has facemasks at each of the corners. It is East Anglian in origin and dates 520-550.

When many of these brooches are first unearthed their gilding can be

AS59
Heavily ornamented large square headed gilt bronze brooch.

CM

AS60
Heavily ornamented large square headed gilt bronze brooch.

CM

covered with green verdigris; in fact, in some cases it will not be possible to see the gilding at all. It requires careful cleaning to bring out the gold appearance.

In the case of the next square headed brooch, **AS61**, which was found near Norwich, no visible signs of gilding were evident. It was only under microscopic examination that it could be determined that gilding existed underneath the encrustation. In fact, as can be seen from the photograph, the gilding was over 95% intact. This is quite an unusual occurrence and it indicates that this brooch had hardly been worn when it was deposited in a burial. It has a trapezoid head plate with decoration consisting of a simplistic facemask comprising two square eyes and a square nose within a rectangular

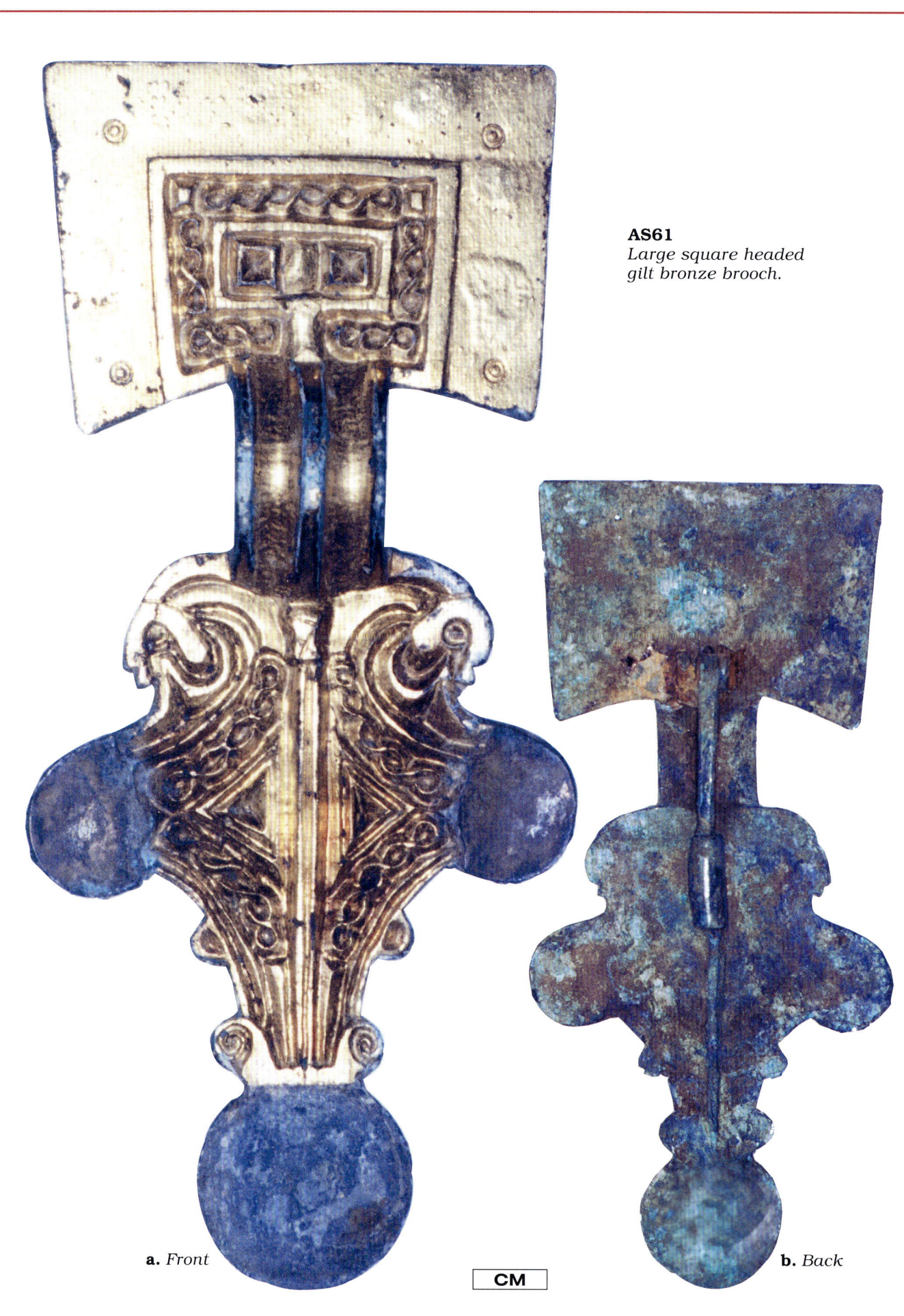

AS61
Large square headed gilt bronze brooch.

a. *Front* b. *Back*

F62
Bronze radiate head brooch.

F63
Gilt bronze radiate head brooch with garnets.

AS64
Small bronze long brooch.

order. This is surrounded by rands of cable moulding. The wide rimeter field is plain except for a ngle ring and dot punch in each rner. The arched bow has three os and the footplate has semi-circular side lobes and a discoid terminal lobe. These lobes, which are flat and undecorated, would originally have had silver foil appliqués. The decoration around the shoulders at the base of the bow consists of animal heads with rounded eyes and open jaws. On each side of a central o is a triangular field bordered by rands of cable moulding matching at on the head plate. **AS61b** shows the back of the same brooch. One of the interesting features is that it has bronze rather than an iron pin. gain a mid-6th century date would ply.

One series of fibula brooch of ankish origin is the radiate head pe, which generally date from the h century when found in England. 2 is a small example with a semi-circular head plate divided into triangular-shaped segments. There is a single projection at the top. The arched bow has a central raised rib. The shortened foot has a zoomorphic terminal with lentoid eyes, and moulded transverse lines above.

A more elaborate example is shown in **F63**. This has a semi-circular head with five projecting terminals; each is of domed outline with two collars. The arched bow has five ribs. The field below has two projecting lobes each inlaid with garnets. The tapering foot is thickened with a simplistic head. The circular eyes are inlaid with garnets. The entire surface of this brooch was originally gilded, of which about 25% remains. The pin, as usual, is of iron but still survives.

Another unusual small long brooch is shown as **AS64**. It has a square head with rounded lobes on each side and at the top. The head plate is decorated with double ring and dot motifs in a figure of five pattern. There is a small ring and dot punch on each of the lobes. The bow is highly arched and quite narrow, while the foot is lozenge shaped with a thickened terminal and two lobes. The double ring and dot motif continues along the foot. This example dates from the late 5th century.

The last fibula type brooch used in Britain in the Anglo-Saxon period is a series of quite small very highly arched equal armed types called Ansate. These are Frankish/Merovingian/Carolingian or Anglo-Saxon and date from the 7th century to the end of the 9th century AD. They are quite prolific finds and represent one of the most popular and inexpensive brooches of this period. They date from the period when pagan burials are no longer encountered, subsequently they are not normally found in graves. One of the characteristics of this type of brooch is that when viewed in profile they resemble a walking caterpillar.

M65 is an example, probably Merovingian, and dates from the 7th-8th centuries. It has simple discoid terminals at each end, a chip carved ornamentation forming a cross in the centre, and straight lines around the edge.

M65
Bronze equal armed brooch.   CM

M66 also dates from the 7th-8th centuries and is very simple in its design. It has the usual highly arched bow, which can be seen in the photograph **M66b**. It is composed of globular segments divided by horizontal beaded ribs.

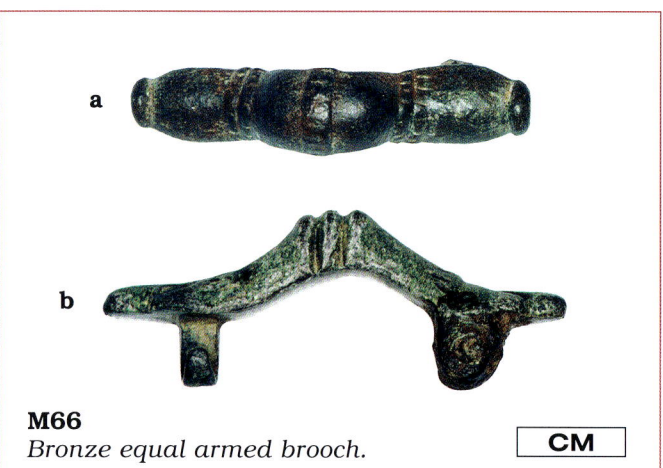

M66
Bronze equal armed brooch.   CM

Another example, **M67** has triangular shaped ends with chip carved decoration, and a lozenge shape in the centre enclosed within an oval band. Interestingly, the ends of this brooch are looped, perhaps for a chain. It would date from the 7th-8th centuries.

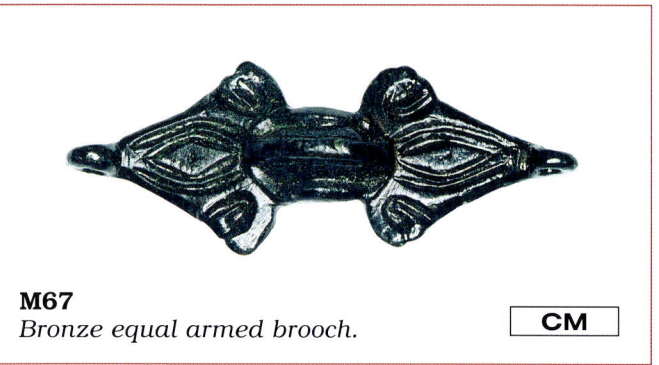

M67
Bronze equal armed brooch.   CM

English examples of this type of brooch are extremely crude. **AS68** has narrow arms with three lateral ribs at the centre of the bow. There are grooves at the end of each arm forming a V-shape with an elongated terminal between.

AS68
Bronze equal armed brooch.   CM

Another very crude example is **M69**. It has a simple decoration of incised V-shaped lines in two bands running down the length of the brooch and making it snake-like in appearance.

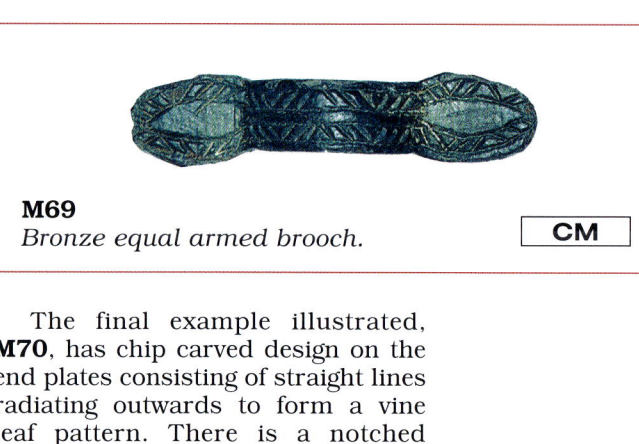

M69
Bronze equal armed brooch.   CM

The final example illustrated, **M70**, has chip carved design on the end plates consisting of straight lines radiating outwards to form a vine leaf pattern. There is a notched design along the edge of the extended bow. This example is probably 7th century.

M70
Bronze equal armed brooch.   CM

Price Guide

		Fine	Very Fine			Fine	Very Fine
AS47	Bronze cruciform brooch.	£30	£70	**AS58**	Gilt bronze square headed brooch with side lappets.	£550	£1300
AS48	Bronze cruciform brooch.	£168	£375	**AS59**	Heavily ornamented large square headed gilt bronze brooch.	£2600	£6500
AS49	Bronze cruciform brooch with side lappets.	£175	£400	**AS60**	Heavily ornamented large square headed gilt bronze brooch.	£2400	£6000
AS50	Large bronze cruciform brooch zoomorphic terminal.	£225	£550	**AS61**	Large square headed gilt bronze brooch.	£1200	£3000
AS51	Large bronze cruciform brooch, facemask terminals.	£850	£2400	**F62**	Bronze radiate head brooch.	£55	£130
AS52	Small bronze long brooch.	£28	£65	**F63**	Gilt bronze radiate head brooch with garnets.	£375	£850
AS53	Small bronze long brooch with side lappets.	£45	£110	**AS64**	Small bronze long brooch.	£40	£95
AS54	Small bronze long brooch with perforated head.	£42	£100	**M65**	Bronze equal armed brooch.	£25	£60
AS55	Small bronze long brooch, trefoil head.	£40	£95	**M66**	Bronze equal armed brooch.	£18	£45
AS56	Bronze Equal armed brooch, trefoil ends.	£75	£220	**M67**	Bronze equal armed brooch.	£45	£110
AS57	Small gilded bronze square headed brooch.	£85	£240	**AS68**	Bronze equal armed brooch.	£18	£45
				M69	Bronze equal armed brooch.	£20	£48
				M70	Bronze equal armed brooch.	£18	£45

Chapter 4

Disc Brooches

During the 5th century AD disc brooches were in everyday use. The most common form is shown as **AS71**. This is of bronze with decoration consisting of a punched double ring and dot motif in the centre, with three more single ring and dot punches equally spaced around this (sometimes referred to as a "bull's eye"). The whole is enclosed within two outer concentric circles.

AS71
Bronze disc brooch.

CM

The brooches were decorated with incised or punched patterns after casting, and the surface was often tinned to give a silver appearance. The average diameter is 36mm. One of the characteristics of the disc brooches of this period is that the edges of the brooches are often notched (see "Celtic & Roman Artefacts" S171). Disc brooches of this type would have been worn in pairs, and the date range would be from early 5th century to beginning of the 6th century. One quite rare variety has an openwork design with a cutout pattern usually representing a swastika.

The other significant forms of disc brooches of this period are called "button" or "saucer" types. They originated in Germany at the beginning of the 5th century. The adaptation of a Roman-style human mask by the Franks and Scandinavians gradually spread throughout Europe. The problem is in deciding the exact dates and how the styles developed. There seems to be differing opinions as to when in the 5th century the styles developed in England. Professor J. Hines in his "New Corpus of Anglo-Saxon Great Square Headed Brooches" calls into question the accuracy of the archaeological dating, especially of button brooches. This is surprising considering the thousands of pagan burials that have been excavated by archaeologists over the last 100 years. How many graves do you need to analyse to obtain the necessary information? One possibility could be to have a computer analysis made of all the pagan Saxon artefacts found in graves in England.

The button brooch, as suggested by its name, is the smallest of all the disc brooches with known examples ranging in size from 14.2mm to 31.9mm. It was a form of brooch that may also have served as a dress fastener. Button brooches have been found in female graves (both singly and in pairs) located at the neck, shoulders, or chest of the skeleton.

The button brooch was used principally in southern Britain and northern France, and was an adaptation by the Anglo-Saxons of the larger disc brooch. The primary design is of a male facemask. **AS72**

AS72
Button brooch, gilt bronze, with facemask.
P - Winchester

CM

is a good representation. It is of gilt bronze with a chip carved design. The face has large cheeks and oval eyes with underlines. The eyebrows and nose together form a "T", and there is a small oval mouth. The hair is represented by straight grooves, indicating that it was swept back. There is a raised outer ring with a shallow upturned rim. This is the most realistic face on a button brooch that I have encountered but there is an earlier form found in Kent. These have a separate upper lip in the design, which is likely to indicate a moustache, and have a diameter of around 30mm. It is difficult to be precise on dating, but on stylistic grounds a date of around AD 475 would seem appropriate.

AS73
Button brooch gilt bronze, with facemask.

CM

Another example **AS73** has a smaller facemask of simpler form. Again it is gilded bronze with chip carved detailing. It has circular eyes with eyebrows that curve round framing the face. The cheeks are smaller than those of the previous example, and the mouth is represented by two straight vertical ridges (which is quite unusual). Again, there is a raised outer ring with an angled rim. On all of these brooches the pin would have been of iron and very rarely survives. I would suggest a date of circa AD 475-500 for this example.

AS74
Button brooch gilt bronze, with crude facemask.

CM

AS74 is another button brooch with an even smaller facemask of extremely crude form. Again the brooch is of gilded bronze with chip carved detailing. It has small circular eyes with underlines, thin straight eyebrows and nose, and a wide straight mouth. This example has plain circular borders and an upturned rim. It would date circa AD 500-520.

AS75
Button brooch, gilt bronze, abstract face.

CM

A very small example of a button brooch is shown as **AS75**. This is again gilt bronze with a very simple chip carved design, and presumably a very abstract head. It has a central straight line representing a nose, no eyes (just arched eyebrows), and the design may indicate the final devolvement of the facemask. This example would date AD 525-550.

Another button brooch **AS76**, which is almost fully gilded, appears to be of a zoomorphic design of very abstract form, with a punch marked border decoration. This can be found on examples of square headed brooches dating circa AD 525. The rim on this piece has been broken by ploughing, which is a common

AS76
Button brooch, gilt bronze, zoomorphic design.

CM

occurrence on the rims of these types of brooches. Pagan burials of this period were often very shallow, and many Saxon graves have been disturbed by farming over the last century.

The larger form of disc brooch, of which **AS77** is an example, is called a saucer brooch. This normally has more of a dished form than the button brooch. The example illustrated shows the most common design used (referred to as a "running spiral"), which has origins in Roman art at the beginning of the 5th century. It has a gilded bronze chip carved design of a central ring and pellet, surrounded by six running spirals. There is a punched circular border with a plain angled rim. This example would date from circa AD 475-525.

Saucer brooches were worn by women and in pairs at the shoulder or breast. They range in size from 24mm to 82mm. Most are found in southern Britain, but they also

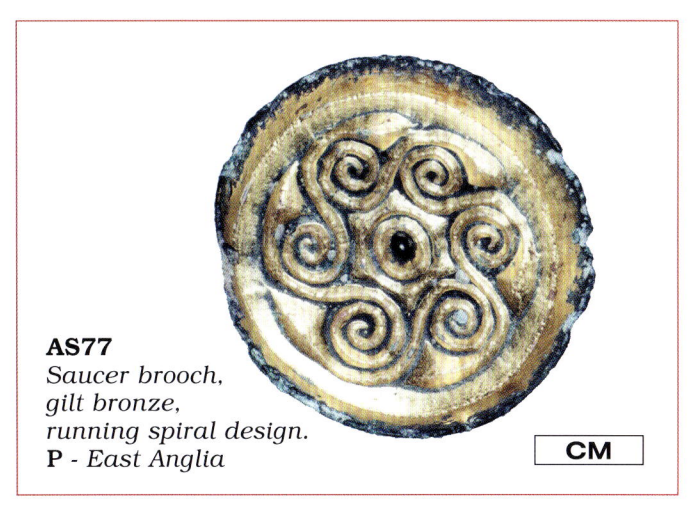

AS77
Saucer brooch, gilt bronze, running spiral design.
P - East Anglia

CM

commonly occur on the east coast up to north Lincolnshire. They are always highly decorated with a chip carved design, either geometric or zoomorphic in form. Very occasionally they can have garnets inset into the centre.

AS78
Saucer brooch, gilt bronze, star design.
CM

AS80
Saucer brooch gilt bronze, with facemask.
P - Kings Lynn
CM

The second most common design after the running spiral is of a star shape, as in **AS78**. Here a central ring and pellet is enclosed by double lines, forming a six-pointed star within a circular border. The rim is upturned. The gilding has worn off on the high points of the design which means that this brooch received quite a bit of wear during use. Again a date of circa AD 475-525 would apply.

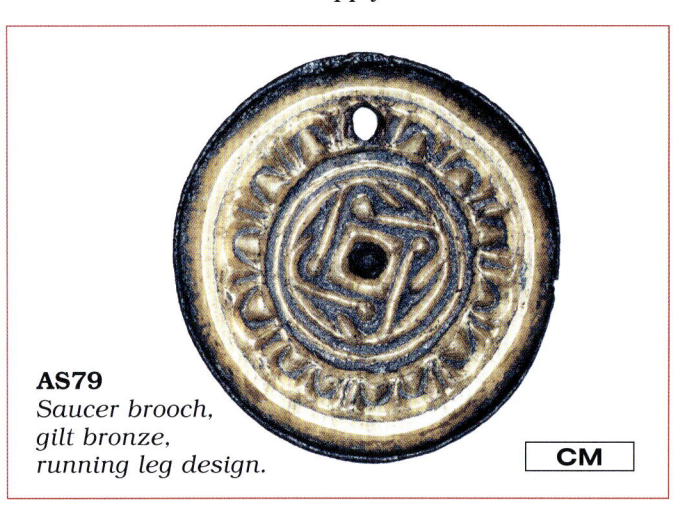

AS79
Saucer brooch, gilt bronze, running leg design.
CM

Another larger example is shown as **AS79**. This has a central pellet surrounded by a running leg design similar to a swastika with barbed ends. This is enclosed within two bands of concentric circles with an outer border of crescents. There is a shallow upturned rim. Interestingly, this brooch has been pierced in the outer border, which indicates that it may have been used as a pendant before being lost or buried. A date of circa AD 500-525 would apply.

The example **AS80** is interesting because it uses a facemask similar to some of the button brooches. The gilding is much lighter in colour than the previous examples. The central design - which is a facemask - has scroll-ended eyes with a curved brow and straight nose of triple lines. This is enclosed within a concentric circle and there is an outer border of triangles. The field between contains straight lines. There is an angled plain rim. This example is likely to date to AD 525-550.

AS81
Small saucer brooch, gilt bronze, cross design.
CM

A very small saucer brooch is shown in **AS81**. It has a central pellet with a triple banded cross within a border of two concentric rings. It has flared rims and I would suggest a date of around AD 525. In some respects it is almost a transitional form between a button and a saucer brooch.

Saucer brooches dating from the early 6th century can be superbly executed. **AS82** is an example, not only in superb condition, but also with a very fine quality chip carved decoration. In the centre is a triskele running leg motif with leg tendrils of feather form. Around this is a field of Style I animals. This style originates in Germanic art around AD 475, and is believed to date in England to around 500-525. The animals' heads are marked with a lentoid eye with crescentic eyebrows and underlines. The bodies are composed of triple stranded ribbon like elements, which

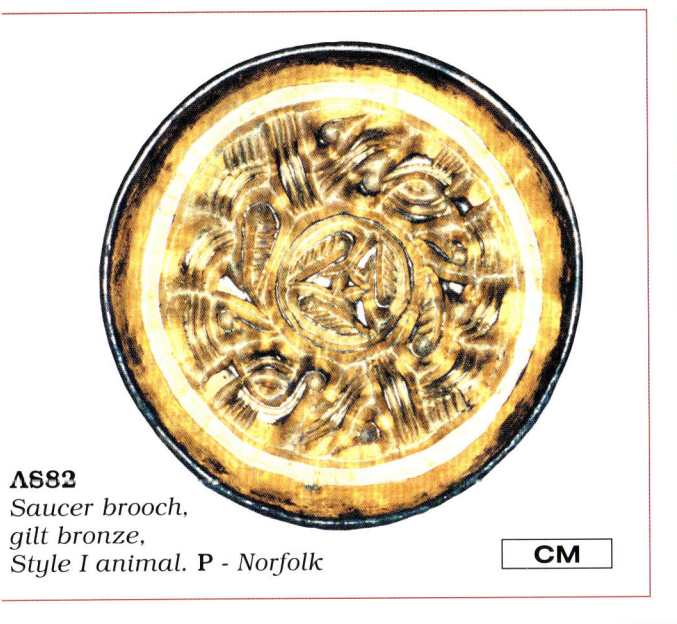

AS82
*Saucer brooch,
gilt bronze,
Style I animal.* **P** - *Norfolk*

CM

AS83
*Saucer brooch,
gilt bronze,
quatrefoil design.* **P** - *East Anglia*

CM

AS84
*Large saucer
brooch,
gilt bronze,
basketry design.* **P** - *Berkshire*

CM

interweave. It represents the finest zoomorphic decoration of this time.

Another saucer brooch, **AS83**, has high flaring rims. The design is heavily gilded with chip carved decoration. There is a central quatrefoil with beaded punched decoration in each arm. This is enclosed in a concentric circle also decorated with beads. The outer field has a simplistic zoomorphic design, which appears to represent limbs. This would suggest a date of AD 525-550.

One of the largest saucer brooches, shown as **AS84**, is intricately chip carved with a central panel of a cross with a pellet in the middle. This is enclosed by a raised circular band outside of which are two sections of basketry ornamentation separated by a concentric ring. This decoration may be a devolved form of Style I animal, which would indicate a date of around AD 575. It has an angled shallow rim.

Another type of disc brooch, again dating from the 5th and early 6th centuries is represented in **AS85**.

AS85
Applied disc brooch, gilt bronze.

CM

AS86
Silver gilt jewelled disc brooch.
P - Norfolk

CM

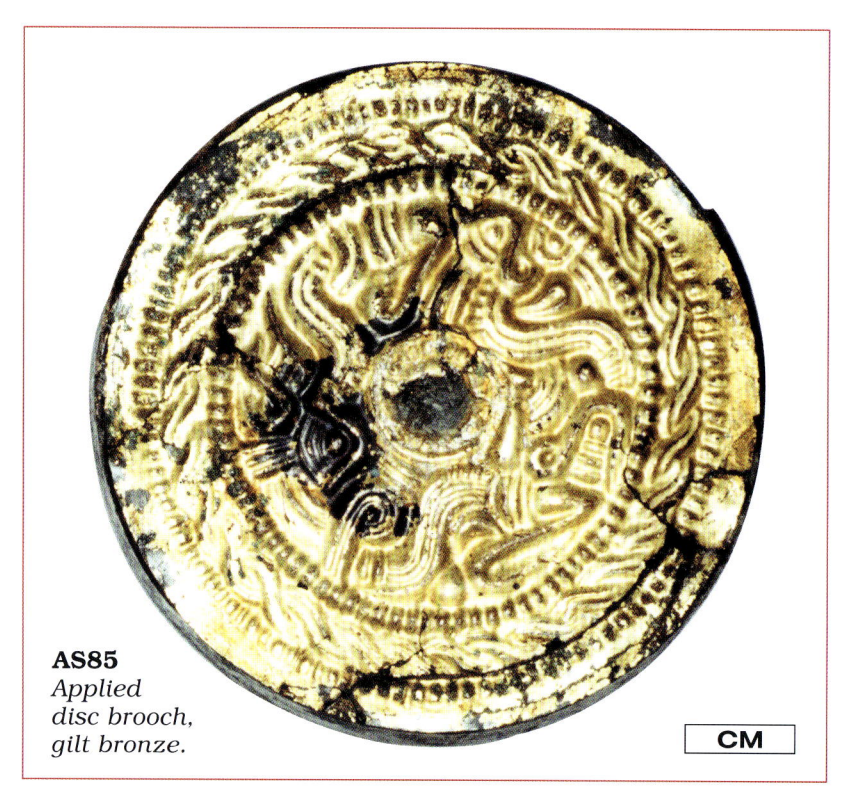

This is called an applied disc brooch. It has a bronze foil of repousse design, which has been gilded. This is soldered at the edges of the rim, which is in turn soldered to the base plate. Some early examples have a very dished base plate on which there is no rim. In the centre there is a hole, which may have originally received a glass inset. The field is decorated with Style I animals with a double band of beaded bordering. Between this is a scroll design. It is likely to date from circa AD 500-525.

The fragility of these brooches, together with the soldering used to apply the foil top means that they rarely survive intact. The example illustrated has, in fact, been restored. The origins of this type of brooch are from Germany during the Roman period of the 4th century.

A much more robust example of a disc brooch is shown as **AS86**. This is a jewelled disc brooch of Kentish origin dating from AD 500-525. It is silver gilded except for a raised border that has niello inlay in a stepped pattern. There is a central circular cell, and three interspaced outer triangular cells each of which would have contained coloured glass, garnets, or a piece of shell. The garnets would have been imported into Britain by the Franks ready to be set into jewellery. The Saxons would usually put gold stamped foil underneath the garnet forming a hatched or latticed effect. This shows the stone to best effect. The field is decorated with Style I animal ornament combined with a realistic male face-mask. The animals have a triple strand ribbon-like body with a crouching leg motif, each leg having three claws.

Jewelled disc brooches were also produced in a composite form. These normally have gold filigree panels between which are cloisonné inset garnets or glass forming a star or cruciform pattern. These have gold-hatched foils underneath to reflect the light through the stones. A base plate, usually of bronze, is cemented in place by the use of plaster with a silver back plate for the attachment of the pin and catch plate. These brooches were first used on the Continent during the late 6th century and the ornamentation can incorporate Style II zoomorphic decoration, which emerged circa AD 560-570 in Germanic art. Some of the finest and most elaborate examples, dating from the early to mid 7th century were produced in Kent.

In the 8th and 9th centuries, pins made of bronze or silver were the primary fasteners in use.

Apart from the equal arm brooches, which were used during the 6th-9th centuries, brooches were no longer fashionable for securing women's clothing.

It was the Viking influence during the 9th century that reintroduced the wearing of disc brooches into Britain. New forms of art were developed, the most common being the Borre style that came to England around AD 865.

V87
Bronze disc brooch, Borre style.

CM

V89
Lead disc brooch, Borre style.
P - Lincoln

CM

V87 is an example of a disc brooch with a flat decorated surface in the Borre style. There is a central circular hollow, which can be inset with a glass stone or gilded. Around this is a lozenge shape with ribbon ends that extend and curl round in a Borre knot motif. There is a central groove creating a double band to the design. It was a mass produced Anglo-Scandinavian cast brooch, sometimes very poorly executed and extensively used throughout eastern England with many examples from East Anglia.

masks have large ears of rounded form. This example dates from the early 10th century.

V91 is another domed disc brooch of heavily gilded bronze with the same triangular-shaped animal masks. In the centre is an expanding cross with the masks situated looking outwards from the ends. This is again of 10th century date and may be a Scandinavian import.

V88
Gilded disc brooch, Borre style.

CM

V90
Gilded bronze brooch with animal masks.
P - Northampton

CM

V88 is a finer quality domed disc brooch of gilt bronze. In the centre is a boss with a cross design, the ends of which intertwine around themselves creating a double knot. This would date from the 10th century when domed disc brooches replaced the flat disc form, which was more common in the 9th century.

An example produced in lead, again using the Borre design, is **V89**. This has a series of ribbon-bodied animals interlacing with one another. Each head has a ring and dot outline forming the eye of the snake-like creature. There is a beaded decoration down each of the animal's bodies.

Another example in gilded bronze is **V90**, which is a domed disc with a central trefoil design. In each angle is an animal mask with pellet eyes and triangular shaped snout. Often the

On the back of these brooches there will be a double lug and catch plate for the placement of the pin but the Scandinavian examples have an additional loop, which is used for the suspension of a pendant. The animal masks are more commonly found on a lozenge-shaped openwork brooch, often of gilded bronze with an animal head in each corner, and these occur

V91
Gilded bronze brooch with animal masks.

CM

V92
Bronze openwork Jellinge style disc brooch.
P - Norfolk

CM

In Scandinavia, from the excavation of pagan Viking burials, it is known that in the 9th to 10th century women usually wore a pair of large oval bronze brooches, which were to fasten clothing at the shoulders. These were of openwork casting with elaborate decoration of interlacing animals. Unfortunately there are only a few known pagan Viking burials in England.

V94 is a very fine circular example of similar form. It is of gilded bronze with a central raised boss supported by four legs, and hollowed out underneath. Around the perimeter are four inward looking facemasks. The field is richly ornamented in a series of Borre style knots with ribbon like bodies with single and double grooves.

A very distinctive form of disc brooch was produced in England during the late 10th and 11th centuries. They were made of gilded bronze with a central field of cloisonné enamel. At first it was believed that these were late Roman in origin but it is now recognised that in the late 10th century cloisonné enamelling was reintroduced to Britain via Germanic and Byzantine art.

AS95 is a good example with most of the gilding present. There are four perimeter lugs, two of which still retain a blue glass bead. The central design is a cruciform motif with a floral aspect of four piriform shaped petals positioned equally around the central concave sided square. As can be seen the colours are essentially two different shades of blue with two petals of yellow.

Another example **AS96** has seven peripheral lugs each set with a glass bead of blue, yellow, or white colour. The central design is of a quatrefoil with four outer petals. Again the colours are predominantly shades of blue with yellow and white as subsidiary colours.

A slightly larger example is **AS97** which has lost most of its gilding. It is unusual in having a scalloped edge with six insets of blue glass beads. The central design is a star-shaped pattern with a red circular centre. The star has a yellow field and there are outer semi-circular panels of blue. As can be seen from the photographs, the glass on all the brooches has survived extremely well. The central panel of enamel is situated in a circular tray, which is set into the framework of the brooch.

On one known example the pin was intact. It was extremely thin and of flimsy construction that suggests that these brooches were intended as

throughout the Viking world. Some English examples made of lead have been found in East Anglia.

A rare example of an openwork domed disc brooch is **V92**, which is of the Jellinge style. This has a beast with an interlacing ribbon-like body, segmented in the middle to form a ladder pattern (a distinctive feature of this style). There is a central rivet connecting the openwork top to a bronze backing plate. This gives a strong three-dimensional appearance. It would date to the late 9th or early 10th century and is a Scandinavian import. Jellinge is one of the rarest Viking art forms to be found on metal artefacts as it was principally used on stonework.

AS93 is an early to mid 10th century disc brooch of flattened form that was produced in England and is a common type. It has a backward looking animal facing its tail, which is forward pointing. Each of the four feet have three claws and around the perimeter are 28 beads (this is the usual number). This is a very good example as many are very poorly cast or show wear from long use. Originally it was thought to be East Anglian in origin but as several examples have been found at the Viking settlement at Coppergate in York, it may have been produced in different areas.

AS93
Bronze disc brooch, quadruped design.

CM

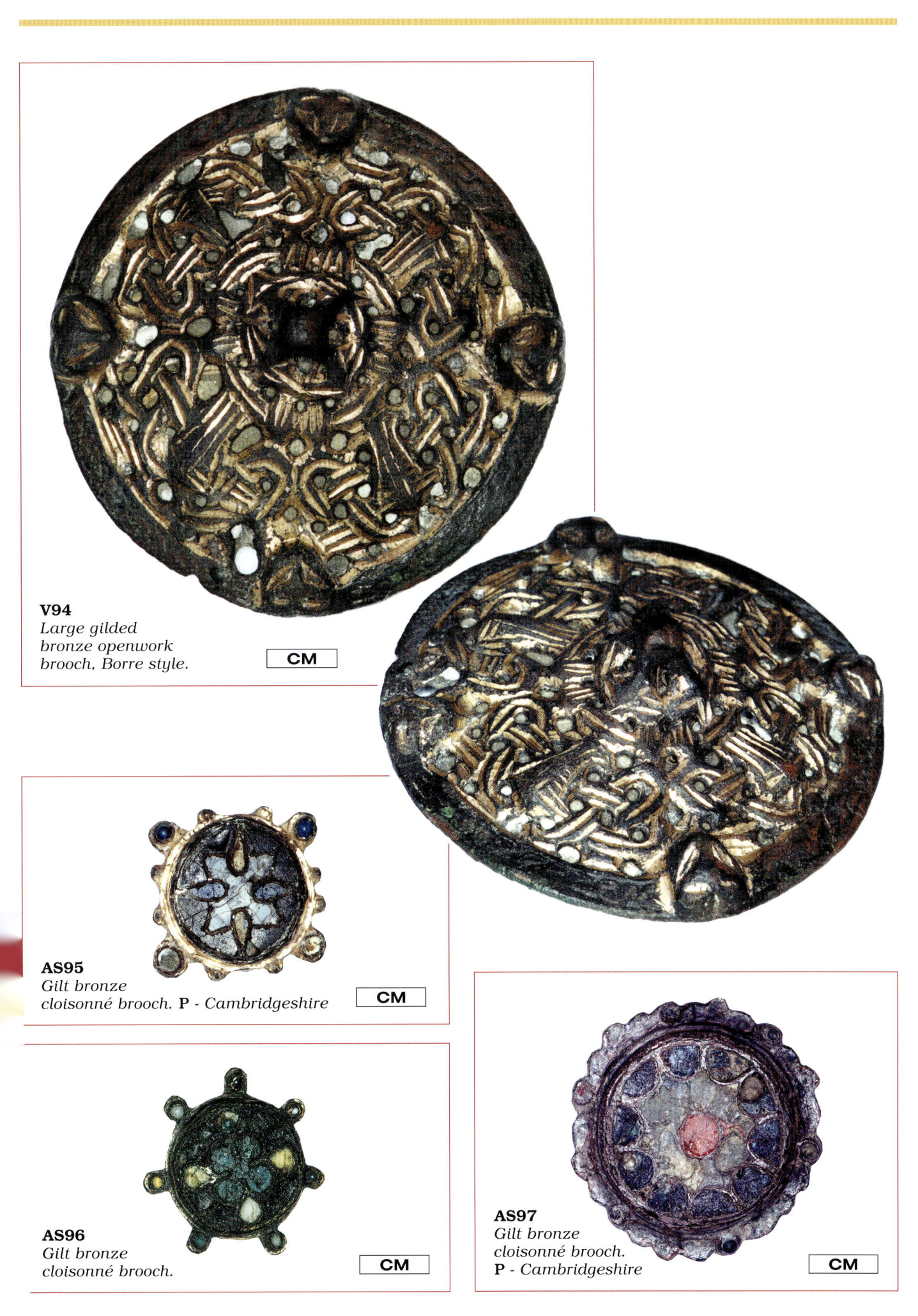

V94
Large gilded bronze openwork brooch, Borre style. **CM**

AS95
Gilt bronze cloisonné brooch. **P** - *Cambridgeshire* **CM**

AS96
Gilt bronze cloisonné brooch. **CM**

AS97
Gilt bronze cloisonné brooch.
P - *Cambridgeshire* **CM**

AS98
Bronze disc brooch, profile male head. CM

AS101
Pewter disc brooch, scroll design. CM

cheap jewellery rather than as functional brooches.

One series of quite obscure disc brooches are shown as **AS98-100**. In the centre is a profile male bust shown looking to the right. The first example **AS98** has a beaded border with a diademed head, probably based on a late Roman bust. The second example **AS99** has a cruder portrait with a pellet eye and small pointed nose. The hair is shown by a series of grooves and around the perimeter are two rows of beading.

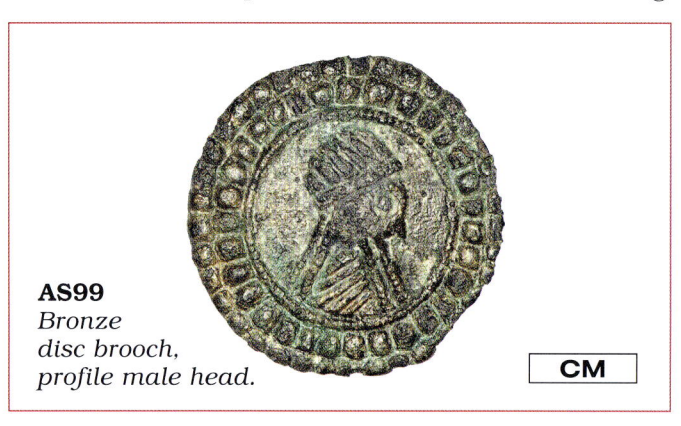

In the 10th and 11th centuries pewter and lead were used to cast disc brooches. A hoard of jewellery found in Cheapside, London contained brooches and rings made of pewter. One of the brooches had a central scroll pattern similar to **AS101**. Here three volutes back to back with scrolled pellet ends, are on a central raised area. The rim is

AS99
Bronze disc brooch, profile male head. CM

AS102
Pewter disc brooch, short cross design.
P - London CM

decorated with a pellet border. The pin is most likely to have been made of iron.

AS102 is a very fine example found in the Thames (hence its clean appearance). Made of pewter, it bears a cross design similar to the short cross pennies of Cnut. This would date it to the 11th century. At this time a number of silver pennies were mounted as brooches with the reverse cross gilded and fixed with a silver pin.

The final example **AS100** has an almost bird-like face with a pellet eye and pointed nose, with very crude detailing. There is a border of three bands of beading. Interestingly the brooch has been gilded although this is very pale indicating that a low quality gold was used. I would suggest a 9th century date for all three examples. They may be late imitations of bracteate or coin pendants, which were regarded as having amuletic powers.

Another example, this time made of bronze, is shown in **AS103**. Made of repousse stamped from a thin sheet, it had an expanding cross in

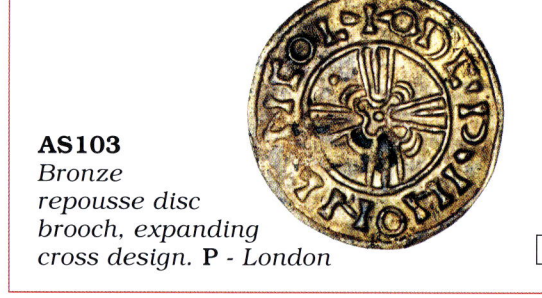

AS100
Gilded bronze disc brooch, profile male head. CM

AS103
Bronze repousse disc brooch, expanding cross design. **P** - London CM

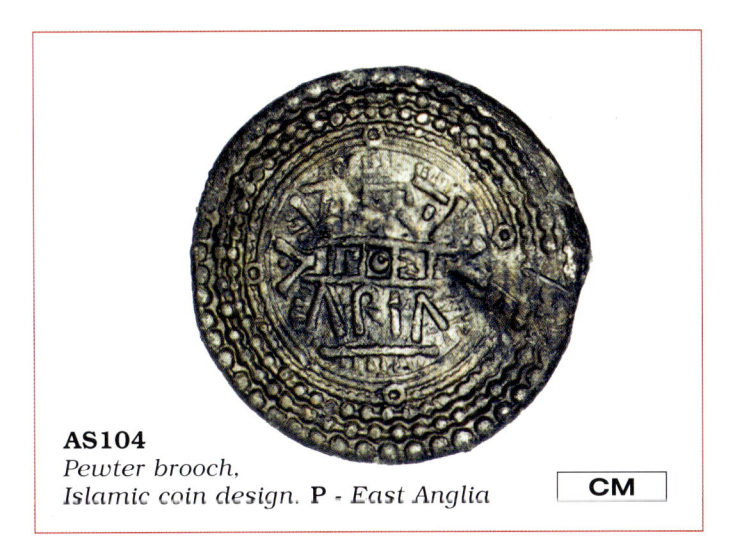

AS104
*Pewter brooch,
Islamic coin design.* **P** - *East Anglia*   CM

the centre with a blundered legend. It may be imitating a coin of Edward the Confessor, which would date it to the late 11th century. The delicate pin is also made of bronze.

When the Vikings arrived in England they brought with them Islamic silver coins called *dirhams*. The pewter brooch shown in **AS104** has a design that seems to imitate the reverse of one of these coins. The perimeter has four beaded bands surrounding the central design of which the letters "ARIA" are visible.

AS105 is a disc brooch in lead with an expanding cross in the centre and circular bands surrounding it composed of billeting and beading. It may be early 11th century in date.

Another example found in the Thames is **AS106**, which has a quatrefoil in the centre on a raised central disc. Around this are bands of beading and billeting. This is likely to be of mid 11th century date.

AS105
*Lead
disc brooch
expanding
cross design.*
P - *East Anglia*   CM

AS106
*Pewter
disc brooch,
quatrefoil design.* **P** - *London*   CM

Price Guide

		Fine	Very Fine
AS71	Bronze disc brooch.	£28	£65
AS72	Button brooch, gilt bronze, with facemask.	£55	£140
AS73	Button brooch gilt bronze, with facemask.	£50	£120
AS74	Button brooch gilt bronze, with crude facemask.	£48	£120
AS75	Button brooch, gilt bronze, abstract face.	£45	£110
AS76	Button brooch, gilt bronze, zoomorphic design.	£46	£115
AS77	Saucer brooch, gilt bronze, running spiral design.	£65	£175
AS78	Saucer brooch, gilt bronze, star design.	£60	£160
AS79	Saucer brooch, gilt bronze, running leg design.	£80	£225
AS80	Saucer brooch gilt bronze, with facemask.	£90	£260
AS81	Small saucer brooch, gilt bronze, cross design.	£55	£130
AS82	Saucer brooch, gilt bronze, Style I animal.	£300	£750
AS83	Saucer brooch, gilt bronze, quatrefoil design.	£260	£600
AS84	Large saucer brooch, gilt bronze, basketry design.	£475	£1200
AS85	Applied disc brooch, gilt bronze.	£350	£900
AS86	Silver gilt jewelled disc brooch.	£1100	£2600
V87	Bronze disc brooch, Borre style.	£60	£150
V88	Gilded disc brooch, Borre style.	£90	£240
V89	Lead disc brooch, Borre style.	£50	£150
V90	Gilded bronze brooch with animal masks.	£70	£180
V91	Gilded bronze brooch with animal masks.	£85	£220
V92	Bronze openwork disc brooch Jellinge style.	£110	£285
AS93	Bronze disc brooch, quadruped design.	£55	£130
V94	Large gilded bronze openwork brooch, Borre style.	£800	£2,500
AS95	Gilt bronze cloisonné brooch.	£95	£260
AS96	Gilt bronze cloisonné brooch.	£95	£260
AS97	Gilt bronze cloisonné brooch.	£95	£260
AS98	Bronze disc brooch, profile male head.	£75	£200
AS99	Bronze disc brooch, profile male head.	£90	£240
AS100	Gilded bronze disc brooch, profile male head.	£85	£240
AS101	Pewter disc brooch, scroll design.	£40	£110
AS102	Pewter disc brooch, short cross design.	£40	£100
AS103	Bronze repousse disc brooch, expanding cross design.	£75	£220
AS104	Pewter brooch, Islamic coin design.	£85	£260
AS105	Lead disc brooch expanding cross design.	£45	£130
AS106	Pewter disc brooch, quatrefoil design.	£50	£140

AS147 *Bronze circular mount, chip carved decoration, Style II Animal, early 7th century.*

Chapter 5

Annular & Plate Brooches, & Dress Pins

One of the simplest types of Anglo-Saxon brooches is of annular form. Such brooches were popular in the late 5th century and throughout the 6th century. They are a more basic version of the quoit brooch, which was used in southern Britain during the 5th century. Annular brooches have been found in women's graves, usually in pairs. They are normally found in East Anglia and along the East Coast of Britain, and have three different forms of pin attachment.

AS107
Annular brooch with pin.   CM

AS108
Decorated annular brooch, without pin.   CM

AS107 is an example in bronze. It has a flat band and a constriction for the bronze pin. The circular band is stamped with a row of annulets in the centre, and it has three equally spaced radial grooves, one of which is for receiving the point of the pin. This example dates from the late 5th century, and is very similar in form to medieval brooch buckles of the 13th and 14th centuries; however, it is far more rare.

The most common method of attaching the pin was by means of a circular perforation in the band (see **AS108**). This example has a wide flat band with an incised decoration consisting of chevrons positioned to create a star pattern. The pin, which in this case is missing, could have been made of bronze or iron. This example again dates from the late 5th century.

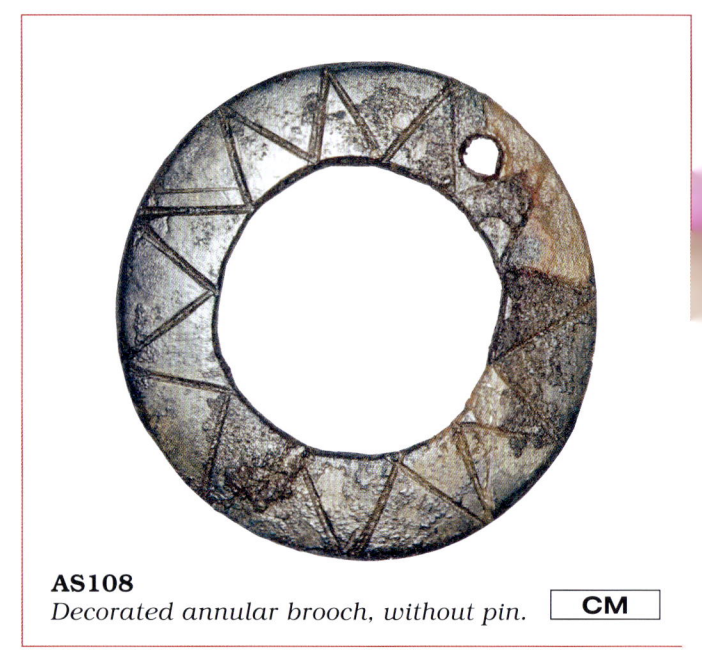

The third type of Saxon annular brooch is shown as **AS109**. It is composed of a flat band decorated with four pairs of radial lines. There is a considerable amount of iron corrosion remaining on opposite sides, representing the remains of the pin. A covering disc was found attached to the brooch, and this is of perfect diameter and form to fit over the top. It is heavily tinned with a repousse punched dot decoration. The pattern is created so that the central dot has eight radial dotted lines with an outer border of dots. The brooch presumably came from a pagan burial that had been disturbed at some time by ploughing.

A series of circular-sectioned rings are also occasionally found in pagan burials. These are too small to be bracelets and may be strap junctions as they are clearly intended for human use. **AS110** has a ribbed decoration, which is interspersed with seven plain beads. A second example, **AS111**, is again heavily ribbed with beaded sections. Neither of the two examples have any traces of corrosion to indicate the presence of a pin, so presumably they are not brooches. I would suggest a date of circa AD 500, and state that these are not common finds.

AS109
*Annular brooch
with repousse cover.*
P - *Norfolk*

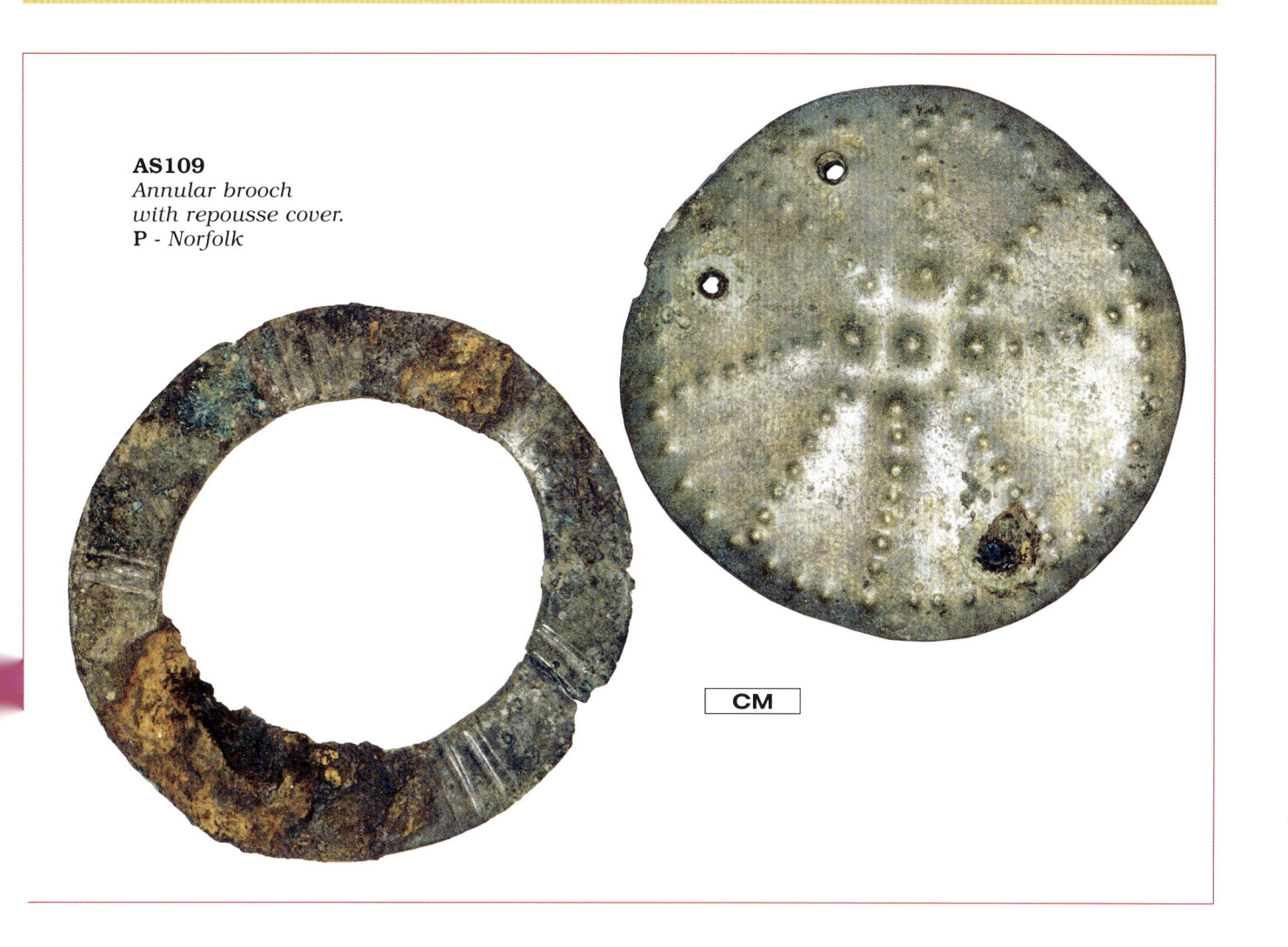

CM

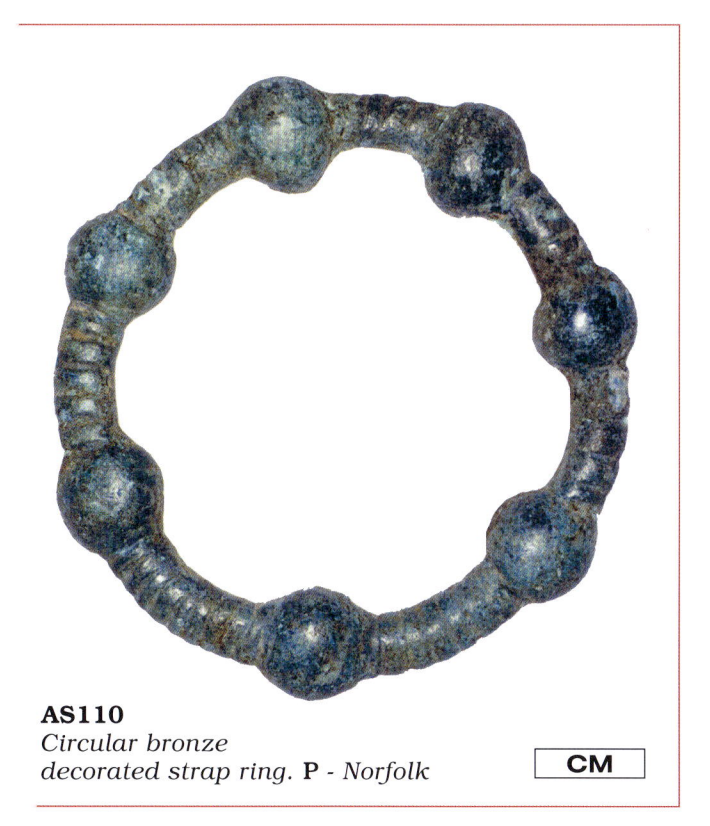

AS110
*Circular bronze
decorated strap ring.* **P** - *Norfolk*

CM

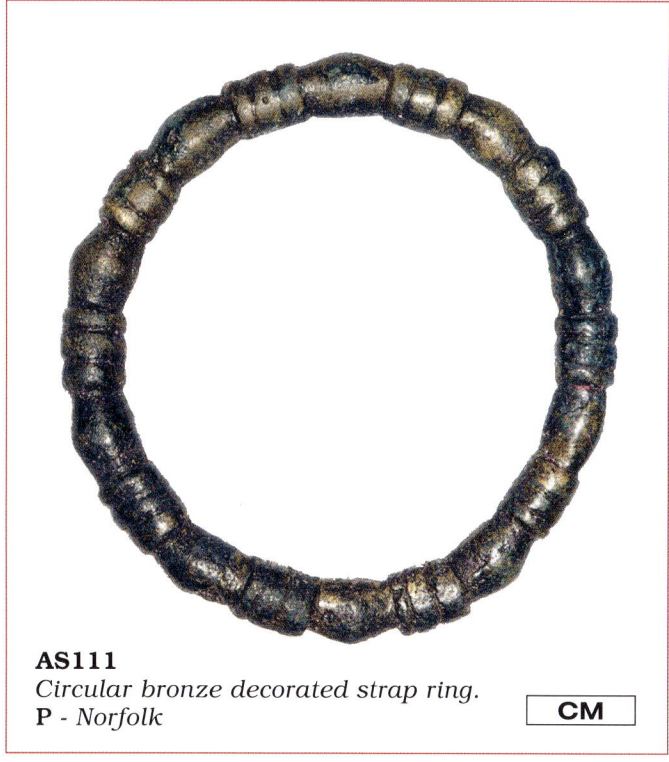

AS111
Circular bronze decorated strap ring.
P - *Norfolk*

CM

AS112
"S" shaped plate brooch,
with animal head terminals. P - Essex **CM**

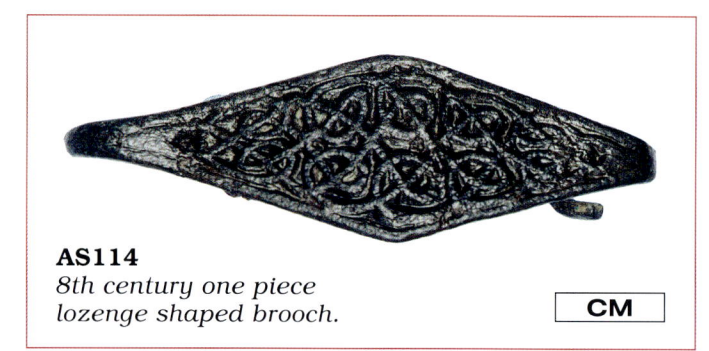

AS114
8th century one piece
lozenge shaped brooch. **CM**

In the 6th century a series of flat plate brooches were produced in Britain, the prototypes of which were originally of Frankish origin. **AS112** is an example that is of an "S" shape with animal head terminals. These are usually birds' heads but on this example the heads are more dog-like. Each animal has a long curving neck with an open mouth and a prominent rounded ear. The eyes are represented by annulet punches, and there are two vertical incised lines on the neck representing a collar. The surface of this brooch is entirely covered in tin plating, giving it the appearance of silver. This brooch would date circa AD 500-550.

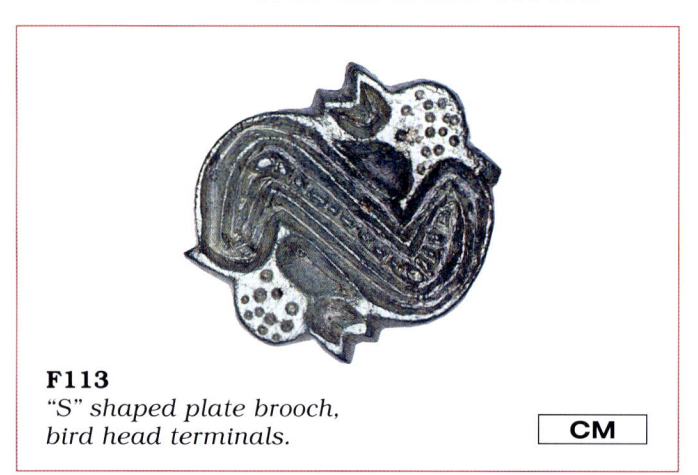

F113
"S" shaped plate brooch,
bird head terminals. **CM**

Another "S" shaped brooch, showing strong Frankish influence, is shown as **F113**. It has two bird head terminals, with punched dot decoration and open beaks. The "S" shaped body has a chip carved design of two lines of grooves and central billeting. This piece would date mid to the late 6th century.

A rare Anglo-Saxon brooch is shown as **AS114**. It is of one-piece construction, made of bronze, and resembles a violin bow brooch of the early Iron Age period. In fact, if it was not for the interlaced design on the flattened bow, it could easily be assigned to that period. However, the very fine chip carved interlaced panel dates the brooch to the mid 8th century. The design consists of latticed ribbon-bodied snake-like creatures, which fill the entire surface of the bow. There are very few brooches that can be accurately dated to this period.

In the late 9th century the Vikings brought to Britain many new forms of brooches. One such type is the trefoil, as shown in **V115**. This was in use from the late 9th to the early 10th century, and the design was copied from Frankish belt mounts. As usual, such brooches were worn by women and primarily used to hold a shawl in place. However, in Scandinavia they were also worn with a pair of oval brooches at the shoulders for supporting an apron-type garment. The example illustrated is typical with its three arms, each with stylised leaf ornamentation. This is set within a tongue-shaped panel. One of the arms of the trefoil is damaged and has been bent. Because of its smaller size, its style and its simplistic pattern this would be Anglo-Scandinavian in origin. Some of the trefoil brooches are richly ornamented in Borre style and gilded, which together with an

V115 Bronze trefoil brooch.
P - Yorkshire **CM**

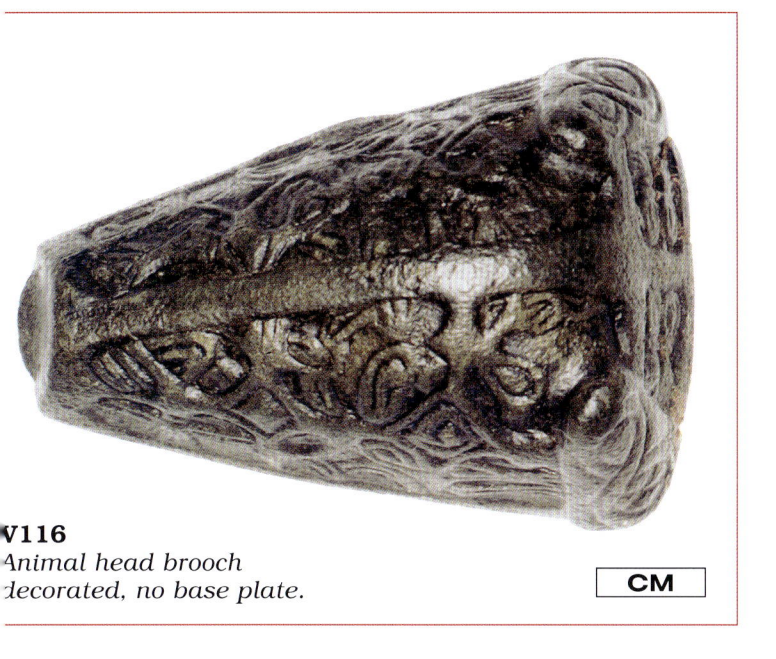

V116
*Animal head brooch
decorated, no base plate.*   **CM**

V118
Plate brooch in form of bird.   **CM**

additional loop on the back, (for hanging a pendant) indicates a non-British form.

Another Viking brooch, which is very rarely found in Britain, is the animal-head type shown as **V116**. This is triangular in shape, hollowed out, and has a separate flat base plate soldered to it. The animal head resembles a boar in profile and is richly decorated with an interlaced design. It dates from the 10th century.

A much later plate brooch in the form of a bird is shown as **V118**. It has a fan-shaped tail and an extended wing, both decorated with straight grooves. The bird is duck-like in the shape of its head and beak. A similar example has been dated to 1020-50.

AS117
*Gilded bronze plate brooch,
eagle form. P - Kent*   **CM**

V119
*Plate brooch
in form of a bird.*   **CM**

A flat plate brooch is shown as **AS117**. This shows a stylised bird (possibly an eagle), which resembles the bird-like ornamentation found on the larger cruciform brooches. It has an extended curving beak, and a triangular-shaped foot and tail. This is scroll ended at the top to form a loop, perhaps for supporting a chain. There are lines of moulding at the head, tail and base. The entire surface is gilded and has a pale gold appearance. This brooch is likely to be Kentish in origin and would date from the late 6th century to the early 7th.

A slightly more decorative bird brooch of bronze with a heavily tinned surface, again of Viking date, is shown as **V119**. It is decorated with ring and dot punches, one of which represents the eye, and there are notches along the edges representing feathers. It has a fan-shaped tail and a narrow upright wing. The head is crested and has a straight beak, indicating a cockerel. There is a hole between the legs, which may have been for receiving a chain. The previous example may also have had this provision, but that part of the brooch is now broken. I would suggest a late 9th or 10th century date.

V120
Silver gilt plate brooch, horseman.

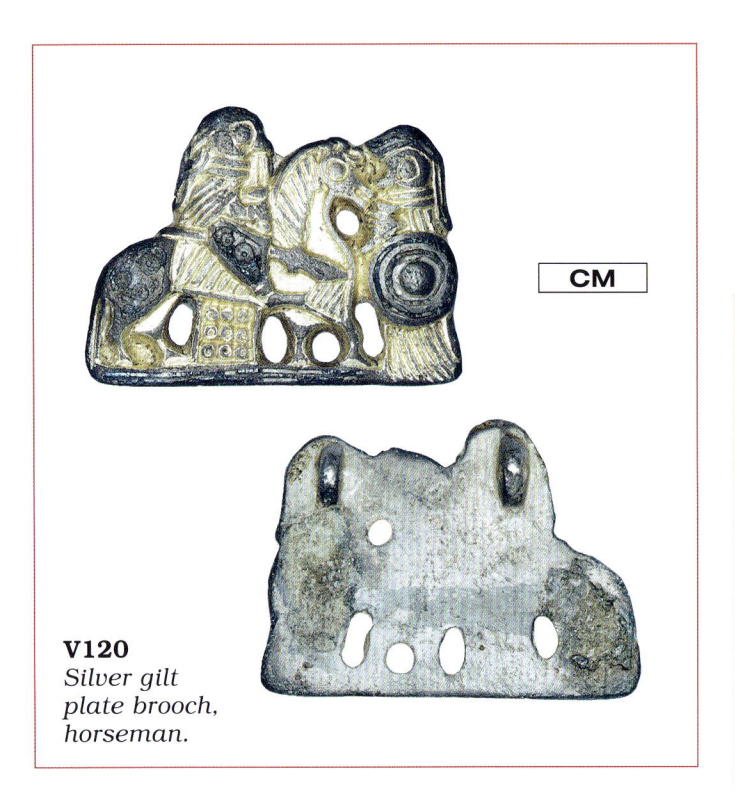

The final Viking plate brooch **V120** is particularly interesting. It is silver gilt and shows a horseman being greeted by a Valkyire (who was one of Odin's followers). She is shown on the right holding a circular shield and a drinking horn to welcome the Viking warrior to Valhalla after his death in battle. This popular scene dates from the late 9th century but is extremely rare in brooch form.

The penannular brooch (which has a gap in the circular loop) was used by the Vikings during the 10th century and worn by men to fasten their cloaks (usually on the right shoulder). These brooches are derived from Irish dress pins. **V121** is an example in silver. It has a twisted loop with scroll ends. The pin is of flattened tapering form with its tip extending past the circumference of the brooch. This is a normal feature of this period.

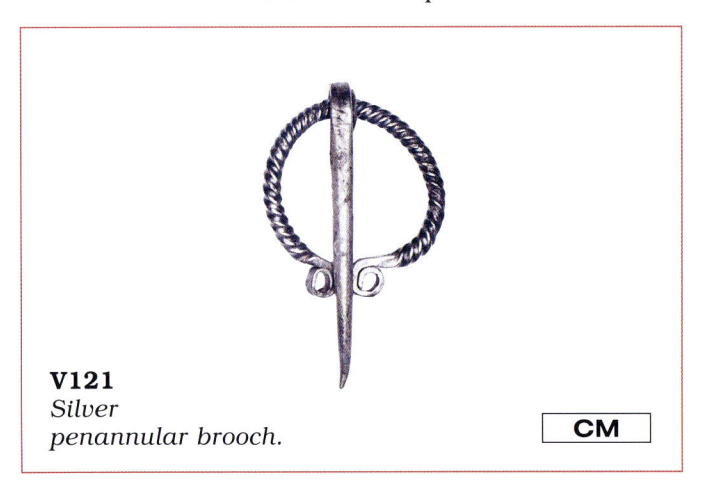

V122
Bronze penannular brooch.

Another example in bronze, **V122**, has animal head terminals to its penannular ring. This type, with its very long fastening shank, could also be classed as a dress pin. It is likely to be Scandinavian in origin, and again dates from the 10th century.

V121
Silver penannular brooch.

Pins

In the early pagan burials of the 5th and 6th centuries very crude bronze pins are occasionally found. The way in which they were manufactured reflects their lowly status at this time. However, during the 8th century the use of pins became widespread for fastening women's clothing. Disc brooches were no longer fashionable and this remained the case until the Vikings reintroduced them in the late 9th century. Small or lightweight pins, in bronze or silver, were likely to be used for pinning veils or other forms of head coverings. The heavier pins were more likely to be used for dresses or cloaks, especially if they have elaborately-decorated heads.

polyhedral head with punched ring and dot design on each of the four sides and also on the flat top. It has an extended thickened collar just below the head, the shank is again of circular section, but on this form there is no bulge. A date of between the 9th and mid 10th century is likely.

A slightly finer example is shown in **AS125**, which again has a polyhedral head but of slightly longer form. Each side is decorated with four symmetrically arranged ring and dot punches, there is a short collar below the pin's head, and there are five incised lines around the middle of the shank, all suggesting a date of 8th to 9th century. This is a longer

AS123
Bronze pin with globular head. **P** - *East Anglia*

AS124
Bronze pin with polyhedral head. **P** - *East Anglia*

AS125
Bronze pin with large polyhedral head. **P** - *East Anglia*

The most common form of bronze dress pin is shown as **AS123**. Cast in one piece, the example illustrated is well finished. It has a long circular sectioned shank with a slight bulge towards the point. This could well have been to prevent the pin slipping while in use. It also has two incised lines around the shank in the area of the swelling. These would also have provided grip. There is a collar just below the pinhead, and the pinhead itself is of solid globular form. The range of dates is likely to be mid 8th to early 10th century.

The second most common form of dress pin is **AS124**. This has a

than normal example, of 10cm length, with a gradually tapering point. On average, dress pins are 5.9cm to 6.4cm in overall length.

Another very common form of pinhead is the biconical, which was especially popular in the 8th century.

AS126 is unusual in having a flat triangular-shaped head with three ring and dot punches, the centre of each being pierced through. The shank of the pin is thicker and slightly flattened, and there is a bulge just past the middle section of the shank. The example is likely to date 9th century.

Another variety is shown in

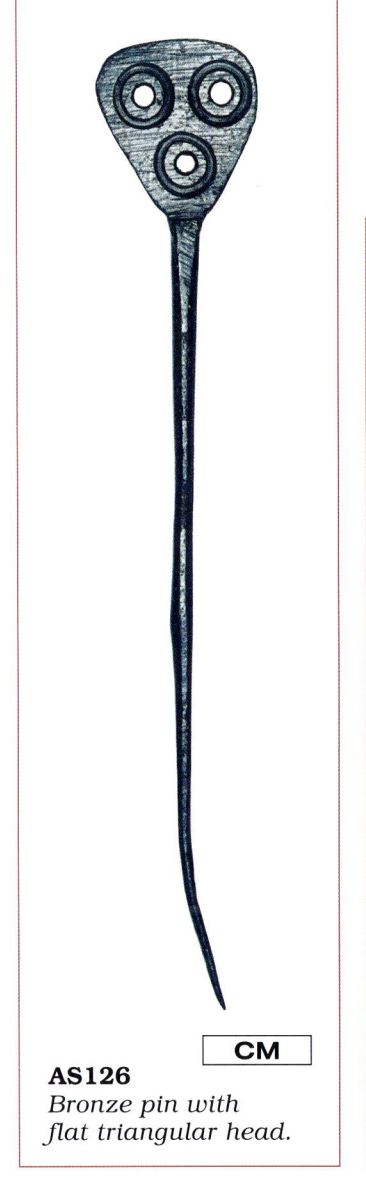

AS126
Bronze pin with flat triangular head.

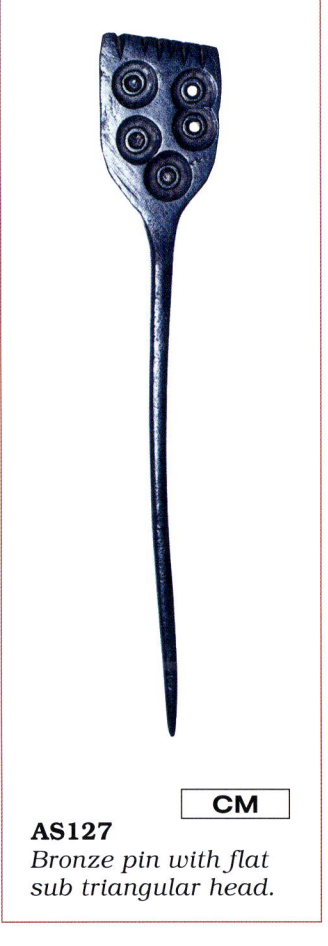

AS127
Bronze pin with flat sub triangular head.

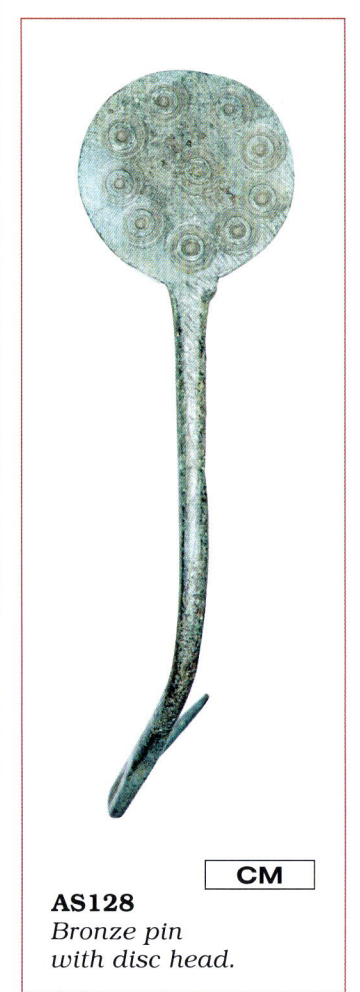

AS128
Bronze pin with disc head.

V129
Bronze ring pin with polyhedral head

AS127. This has a flat head of sub triangular form, with five ring and dot punches arranged randomly. The top edge has six notches, and the shank of the pin is square sectioned. This example is again likely to be 9th century in date.

In the late 8th and early 9th century pins were fitted with separately cast disc heads. These could be intricately chip carved with an interlaced design surrounding animals. They were gilded and sometimes linked together in pairs or triples. The links are elongated strips with pierced terminals. These were connected to the pins by means of wire loops.

AS128 is an example of a disc headed pin with a simple design of punched ring and dots arranged in a circle around a central ring and dot. The thin disc head is attached to a thicker shank that is of square section. There is a bulge on the lower part of the shank. The likely date is late 8th to early 9th century.

Other forms of pinhead include the spiral headed, which date from the 8th to the 11th century, and were sometimes worn in pairs.

During the 9th to 10th century pins were produced with a separate ring that was fixed through the pinhead and swivels around it as shown in **V129**. The pinhead itself is polyhedral and decorated on each face with a panel of raised dots arranged symmetrically to match the design on the ring. The pin shank is heavy duty and of circular section. This is one of the most common forms, especially of the Viking occupation period in England and Ireland (which is where the type originated).

Price Guide

Code	Description	Fine	Very Fine
AS107	Annular brooch with pin.	£30	£80
AS108	Decorated annular brooch, without pin.	£25	£50
AS109	Annular brooch with repousse cover.	£35	£90
AS110	Circular bronze decorated strap ring.	£30	£70
AS111	Circular bronze decorated strap ring.	£28	£65
AS112	"S" shaped plate brooch, with animal head terminals.	£45	£130
F113	"S" shaped plate brooch, bird head terminals.	£50	£140
AS114	8th century one piece lozenge shaped brooch.	£45	£135
V115	Bronze trefoil brooch.	£90	£225
V116	Animal head brooch decorated, no base plate.	£125	£280
AS117	Gilded bronze plate brooch, eagle form.	£120	£275
V118	Plate brooch in form of bird.	£60	£140
V119	Plate brooch in form of a bird.	£85	£200
V120	Silver gilt plate brooch, horseman.	£850	£2400
V121	Silver penannular brooch.	£90	£200
V122	Bronze penannular brooch.	£45	£120
AS123	Bronze pin with globular head.	£12	£25
AS124	Bronze pin with polyhedral head.	£12	£25
AS125	Bronze pin with large polyhedral head.	£20	£50
AS126	Bronze pin with flat triangular head.	£24	£60
AS127	Bronze pin with flat triangular head.	£26	£70
AS128	Bronze pin with disc head.	£30	£90
V129	Bronze ring pin with polyhedral head.	£36	£110

Chapter 6

Keys, Spoons, Hanging Bowl & Casket Mounts

KEYS

In the late 5th and early 6th centuries women wore a pair of ornamental bronze keys, called "girdle hangers" suspended from a belt or a girdle. **AS130** is a typical example, having a long rectangular shank at the end of which are two arms. These arms have concave sides and return at right angles to terminate in two circular lobes. Additionally, there are two semi circular lobes on the lower edge. At the top of the shank is a pierced transverse suspension loop, which may have been connected by an iron link to a matching girdle hanger. This identical pairing occasionally occurs and means that girdle hangers would not have served a practical purpose such as keys or latch lifters. They are often decorated on one side with incised lines or stamped dots, and may also have ornaments suspended from the two arms. They are especially common finds in female graves in East Anglia. The most logical explanation for their purpose is that they were symbolic keys showing the married status of a woman.

After the Romans had left Britain, the use of bronze keys did not reoccur until the 8th century. This was probably due to the rise of Christianity and the building of stone churches and monasteries, which needed locks to protect their religious treasures. One of the characteristics of the surviving keys from the 8th and 9th centuries is the openwork decoration on the bow principally consisting of a cross motif.

AS131 is a very small and simple bronze key with a lozenge-shaped bow of solid form with a central ridge and a short circular shank. It has a long narrow square section tongue positioned at right angles to the shank with a small side projection at the base. It is likely to date from the 8th century.

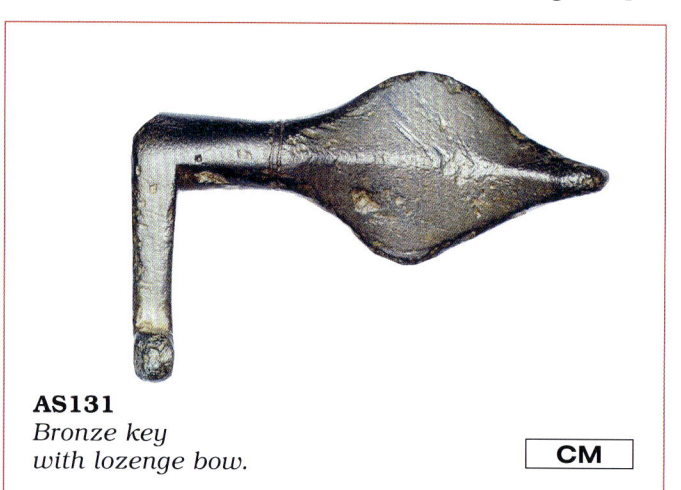

AS130
Bronze girdle hanger.

AS131
Bronze key with lozenge bow.

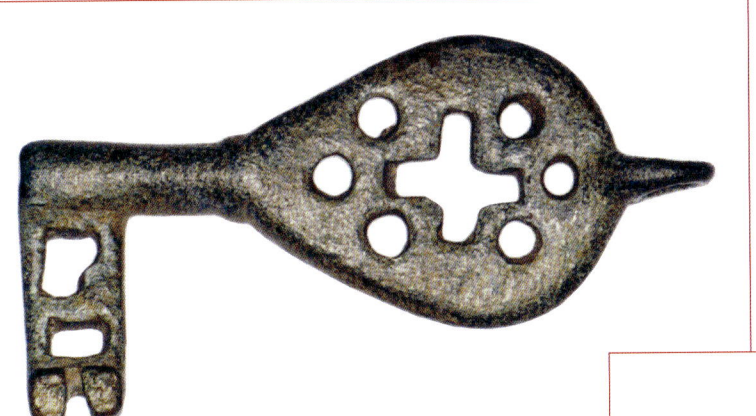

AS132
*Bronze key
with openwork bow.*

CM

AS132 is a more elaborate and larger bronze key, likely to date from the 8th or 9th centuries. It has an openwork shield-shaped bow with a crude cross design in the centre, and three circular piercings above and below this. There is a transverse suspension loop at the end of the bow and the shank is short and circular. The tongue has two piercings and is quite wide; it has two side projections at the base.

Another example, **AS133**, has a circular shaped openwork bow with a cut-out cross design, and a small suspension loop at the end. The short shank is circular in section and thicker than the bow. The tongue has two rectangular piercings and is knobbed on one side.

A larger heavier duty key, likely to be 10th century in date, is shown as **AS134**. It has a circular bow with a cut-out design of seven equally-spaced crosses. Additionally, around the outside of the bow are five rectangular piercings. There is a circular moulding at each end of the bow, with a transverse suspension loop at one end. A separate bronze ring passes through it and is still in position. The circular section shank has a wide tongue with two L-shaped piercings. The key has been fitted with both a replacement shank and suspension loop in antiquity. This is indicated by the fact that the openwork design of the bow has been partially filled in by the brazing process. Whether this is because the existing key had worn out or was simply changed is uncertain, but clearly the ornamental bow was retained perhaps because the design indicated a specific function for the key.

AS133
*Bronze key
with openwork bow.*

CM

AS134
*Large bronze key
with cut-out bow.*

CM

AS135
Bronze key with annular bow. **P** - *Suffolk*

CM

The bronze key in **AS135** has a fine annular ring bow ornamented with an incised ring and dot pattern. The shank is slightly longer than the previous examples, while the tongue is tapering and of square section. I would suggest a date of 10th century for this key. The short shanks of the previous keys appear to be a characteristic of the 8th and 9th centuries, and indicate a shallow receiving lock perhaps fitted to a chest.

suspension loop, through which passes an iron loop that still remains in place. The transverse key bit is made of iron and slots into the shank. It is of thin rectangular section with three cut-outs. The iron has survived because the key was found in anaerobic conditions on the Thames foreshore.

Another late Viking/Norman key dating from the 11th or 12th centuries is shown as **V137**. It is

V136
Key with decorated brass shank. **P** - *London*

CM

Some of the keys from the late 8th and early 9th centuries have confronting animal heads on an oval-shaped bow. Viking keys are also decorated with animals in the form of gripping beasts and usually have a circular bow. **V136** is likely to be of 10th century date and has a brass shank with an expanded waist. It is decorated with a bird in flight design repeated three times. There is a zoomorphic terminal on the integral

made of iron with a bulbous circular section shank with a brass wire inlaid spiral as decoration. There is an integral transverse suspension loop with a collar below. The key bit is transverse, flat in section, and has two cut-outs, one of which is cross-shaped. This type of key was for use on padlocks of box form.

Examples without the brass or copper inlay are more likely to be Norman in date.

V137
Iron key inlaid with brass decoration. **P** - *London*

CM

SPOONS

Anglo-Saxon and Viking spoons are extremely rare. Early examples copy late Roman and Byzantine styles and are predominantly Mediterranean imports. In the 9th century it was usual to have a spoon bowl at one end with a fork blade at the other. These are called "sucket" spoons. General-purpose spoons were normally of wood or bone with a carved design. The bowl is of spatula form (ie long and narrow). **AS138** is an example in bronze with a spatula-shaped bowl decorated on the underside with ring and dot punches. There is a double moulding where the bowl joins the handle, which is circular in section. There are three horizontal lines of incised decoration in the middle, and two at the top where there is a transverse suspension loop. This spoon is likely to be of 9th or 10th century date.

Spoons of this period usually have a zoomorphic head at the junction of the bowl and handle, but are without the step that occurs on Roman spoons.

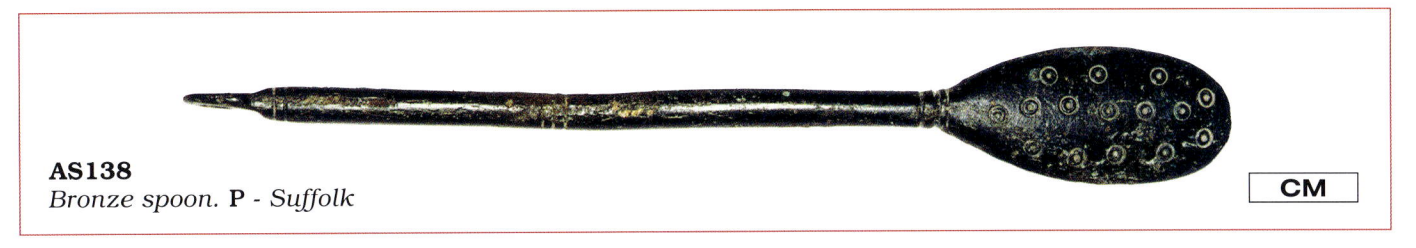

AS138
Bronze spoon. **P** - *Suffolk*   **CM**

MOUNTS

From the mid 6th century through to the early 7th century, a wide bronze bowl with a narrow rim and concave neck was extensively used in Britain and Ireland. Equally spaced around the outside of these bowls, and just below the rim, were positioned three suspension loops. **AS139** is a disc mount that would originally have been attached by solder to such a hanging bowl. It is ornamented with a triskele of spirals, and in the recessed background are traces of decayed enamel. It dates from the late 6th or early 7th century. It has a plain flange, which would have been enclosed within a circular frame.

Another disc mount, shown as **AS140**, is decorated with six connected spirals arranged in pairs. It could also be from a hanging bowl and dates from the early 7th century.

A number of hanging bowl mounts

AS139
Bronze hanging bowl mount.   **CM**

AS140
Bronze hanging bowl mount.
P - *East Anglia*   **CM**

AS141
Bronze hanging bowl mount. **P** - *Somerset*   **CM**

AS142
Bronze hanging bowl mount. CM

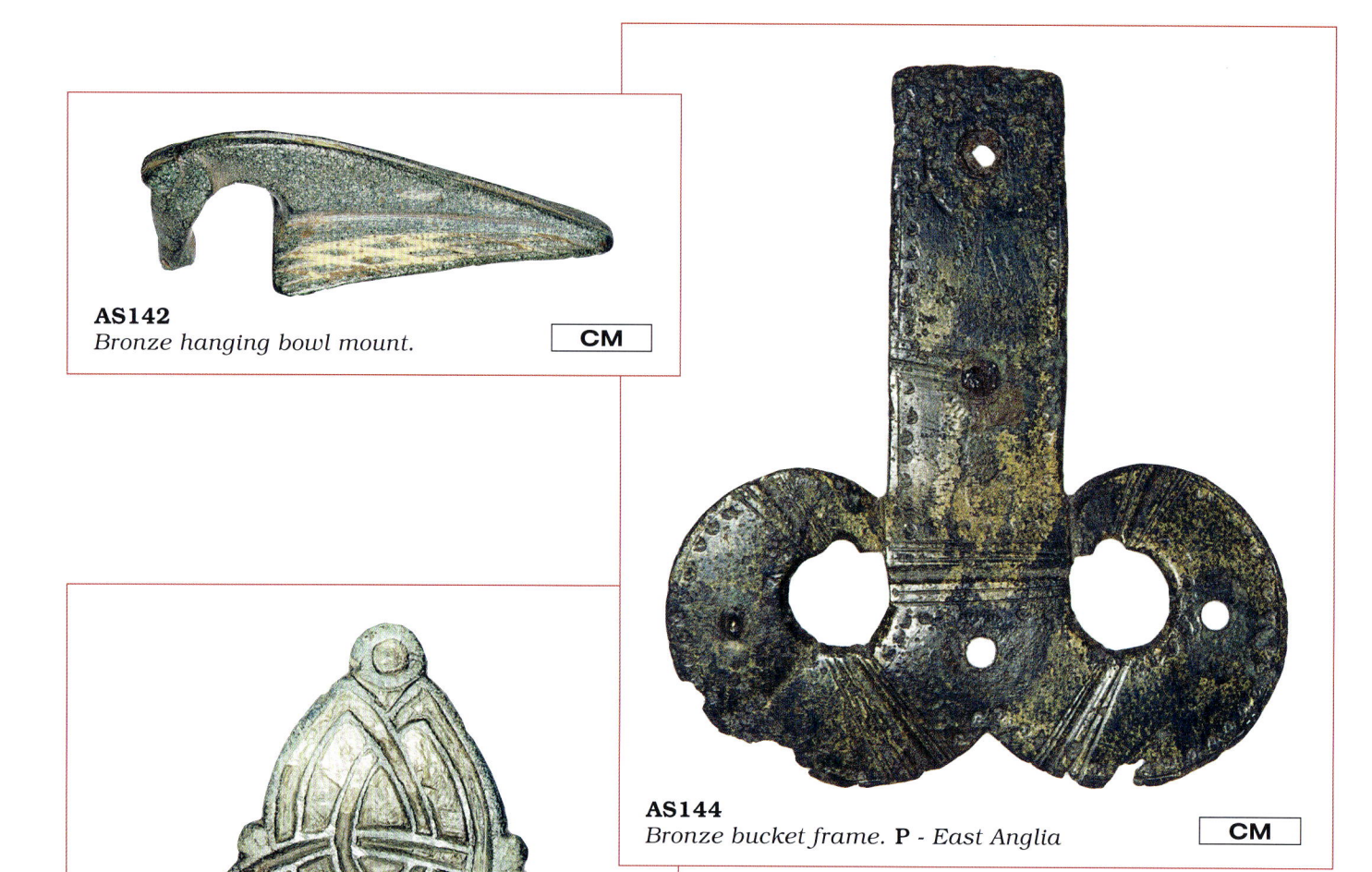

AS144
Bronze bucket frame. P - East Anglia CM

AS143
Bronze trefoil bucket mount. CM

have animal head terminals at the top. **AS141** is an integral mount with a zoomorphic head forming the loop for the handle attachment. The head would have been soldered to the rim of the bowl, and has three additional fixing holes for rivets on the triangular shaped lower plate.

Another triangular-shaped hanging bowl mount with a well-modelled horse's head suspension loop, is shown as **AS142**. There is a cross-hatched decoration on the plate, which may have originally been enamelled.

Another mount, shown as **AS143**, is of trefoil shape and has an interlaced pattern forming three knots; it may date from the 8th-9th century and could have been intended for monastic or religious usage. There are traces of red enamel in the recesses in the field. This could have been a bucket mount. Wooden buckets made from yew are found in a few burials, most commonly male. The metal framework (usually bronze sometimes of iron) is often all that remains.

AS144 is part of the bronze framework of a wooden staved bucket dating from the 6th century. It is the handle escutcheon plate, which has a vertical bar with side lobes at the base. These are of two bird-like creatures with curved beaks. It is made from sheet metal with a punched design of straight grooves and a border of crescents. Rivet holes form the birds' eyes. There would have been two handle escutcheon plates, four upright plates, and three horizontal plates supporting the wooden bucket. These buckets are not particularly large and may have had a ceremonial function.

During the 8th-9th centuries portable house-shaped shrines, of rectangular form and made of wood with bronze frames and hinged lids, were used as Christian reliquaries. They are decorated with applied circular and rectangular gilt-bronze mounts on each side. There can be as many as 12 of these mounts on one shrine. Some have red enamel

AS145
Bronze rectangular mount. CM

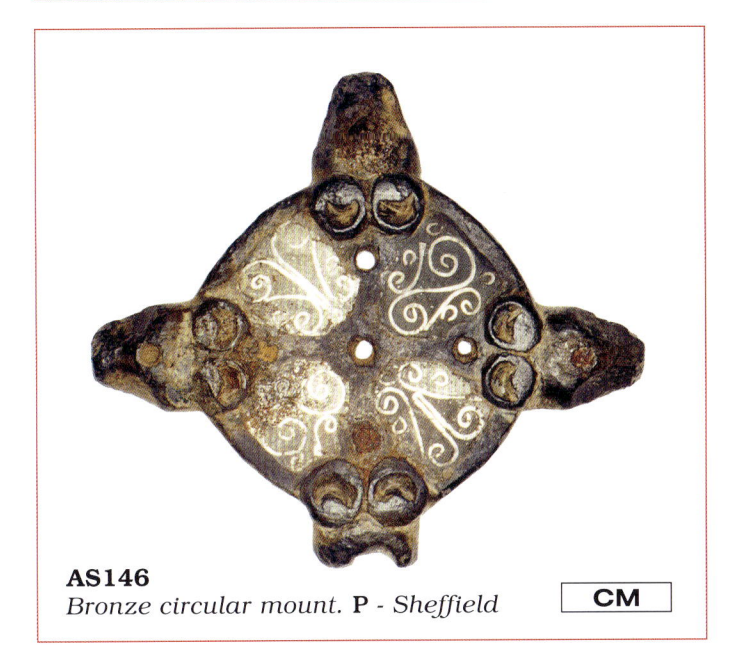

AS146
Bronze circular mount. **P - Sheffield** CM

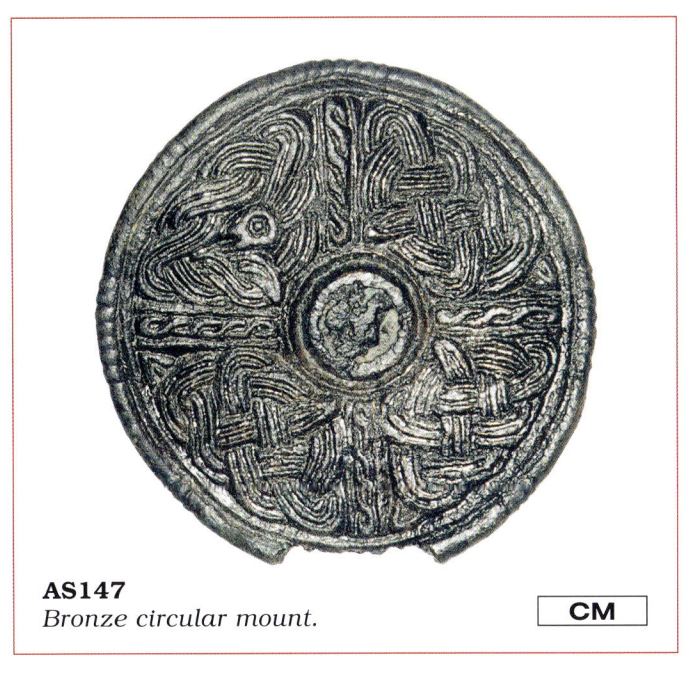

AS147
Bronze circular mount. CM

AS148
Gilt-bronze rectangular mount. CM

AS149
Gilt-bronze circular mount. CM

panels and a central setting of a glass or garnet stone usually with an interlaced pattern in the field. **AS145** is a fairly simple bronze mount of rectangular form dating to the early 8th century. It has an interlaced pattern comprising snake-like ribbon bodied beasts. There is a circular rivet hole in each of the corners.

A bronze circular mount dating from the 9th century is shown as **AS146**. It is of circular form with four outward-facing zoomorphic heads. There is a silver niello inlay of S-scrolls and tendrils inset into the central disc. There are four rivet holes in the centre, with an additional rivet hole through each head.

An earlier bronze circular mount **AS147** is beautifully decorated with a chip-carved Style II Animal design with a triple-stranded body. There is a central circular setting, possibly for a glass or garnet stone, and there are four separate panels of interlace divided by a chain link strip that forms a cross pattern around the central setting. It dates to the early 7th century.

A gilt-bronze mount of rectangular form, shown as **AS148** is again decorated with chip-carved Style II interlaced animal design with a twin-stranded body. It dates to the beginning of the 8th century and has two integral bronze rivets at the back.

Another disc mount, **AS149**, is of gilt bronze with an interlace of Style II Animal that has a triple stranded ribbon-like body. There is a central rivet hole for attachment.

65

AS150
Bronze triangular mount. CM

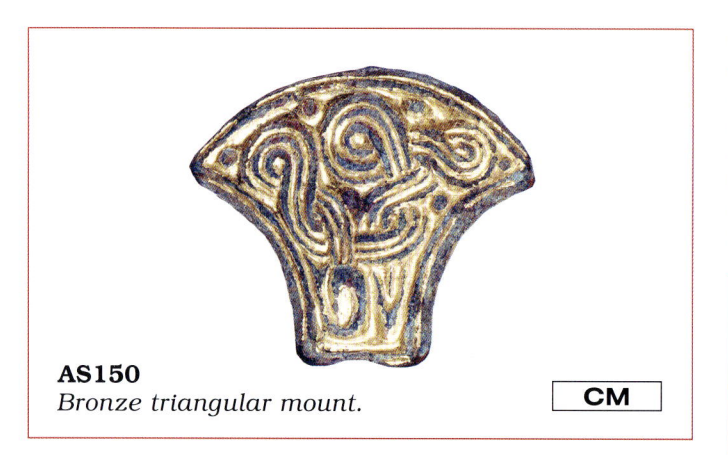

A series of sub-triangular mounts (**AS150**) usually of Style II Animal pattern are typical forms that may represent one arm of a cross. This could have been part of a harness mount that was fitted to the leather straps around a horse's head. There are three integral rivets on the rear.

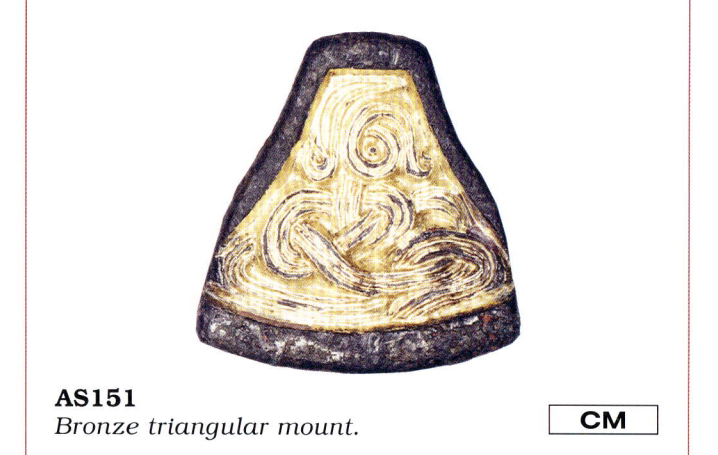

AS151
Bronze triangular mount. CM

A finer quality chip-carved sub-triangular mount (**AS151**) has a triple stranded ribbon snake-like body decoration in a recessed panel, again of Style II Animal design. This would date early 7th century.

An earlier gilt-bronze disc mount

AS152
Gilt bronze disc mount. CM

with a chip carved zoomorphic design with Style I Animal decoration is shown as **AS152**. This dates from the mid 6th century. The central circular boss imitates the garnet settings from the Kentish brooches. The raised border is decorated with ring and dot punches.

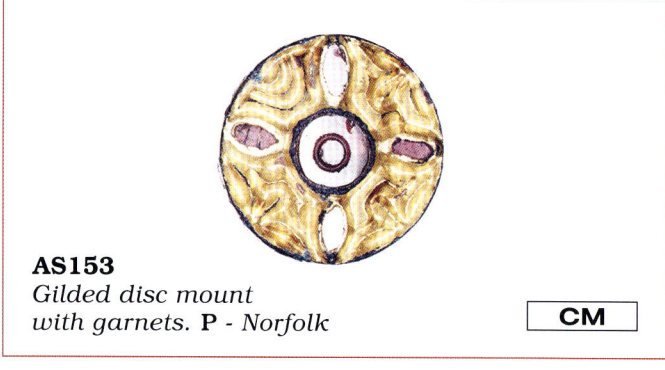

AS153
Gilded disc mount with garnets. **P** - *Norfolk* CM

Another gilded disc mount, again with Style I Animal decoration is shown as **AS153**. This may be an inset from a larger brooch or mount. It has a central circular setting with a garnet that has an annular groove cut into its surface as decoration. Equally spaced around this are four oval-shaped garnets forming a cross of floral design. The lack of a raised border indicates that the mount was enclosed within a separate framework. The fact that the gilding is intact and there is no wear suggests that this mount may not have been used. This mount would be early 6th century in date.

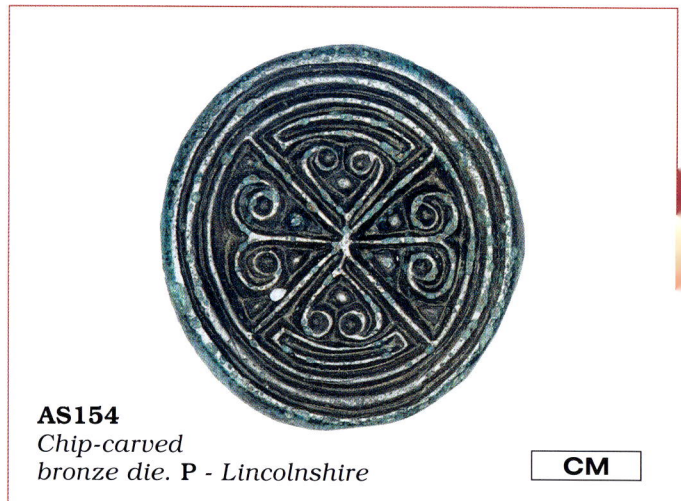

AS154
Chip-carved bronze die. **P** - *Lincolnshire* CM

The heavy bronze disc shown as **AS154** has a deeply-cut design of a scroll-ended cross within a circular border. Rather than being a mount it is possible that this is a die for stamping repousse work. It would date from the early 6th century.

A series of anthropomorphic mounts have been found in southern

AS155
Silver-gilt facemask. **P** - *S Yorkshire*

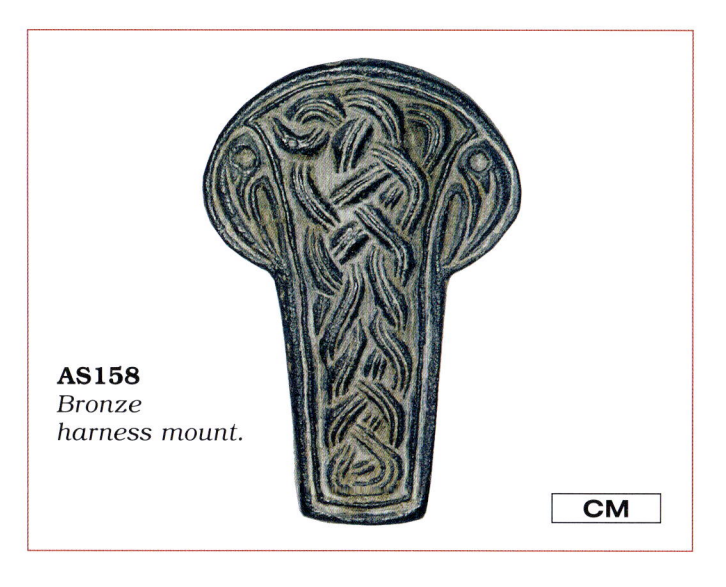

AS158
Bronze harness mount.

Britain. The early 7th century Sutton Hoo burial contained decorations of human head form mounted on the side of a sceptre. **AS155** is a very fine silver gilt shield-shaped facemask representing a mature man. It has a moustache and long beard, and the swept back hair is represented by straight grooves.

AS156
Gilt-bronze facemask.
P - *Cambridgeshire*

A very fine bronze harness decoration dating from the early 7th century is shown as **AS158**. The central rectangular panel shows an interlaced triple banded snake-like creature. On each side of this at the top is a semi-circular panel containing a bird-like creature with large circular eyes and a pointed beak.

AS159
Gilt-bronze mount.

A much cruder example but of similar form is shown as **AS156**. Again the representation has a long pointed beard with a moustache that is scroll ended. The eyes are circular with underlines and arched eyebrows. This is reminiscent of the facemask on button brooches dating to the late 5th and early 6th centuries.

It is possible that these two mounts are intended to be representations of the same god, possibly Woden (who was later called Odin).

The very small intricately decorated bronze mount of triangular shape shown as **AS157** dates from the 8th century. It portrays a beast with an interlaced body, a long curving neck and circular eye. This could be a mount from one side of a sword pommel.

A very rare chip-carved gilded bronze mount of lozenge shape is shown as **AS159**. It dates to the late 8th century and shows a quadruped, probably a horse, surrounded by an interlacing pattern and an outer border of zigzag lines. Although the piece is damaged on one side, from its very thin fabric and small mounting holes it may well be a link, perhaps between ornamental pins.

A similar gilt bronze lozenge-shaped mount again chip carved, also dating from the late 8th century, is shown as **AS160**. This mount again has an interlacing pattern but this time with four square panels each set with a very crude animal head with oval ears. The top mounting hole has a circular suspension loop fitted to it, which may indicate that this item was

AS157
Small triangular bronze mount.

AS160
Gilt-bronze mount. **CM**

AS161
Gilt-bronze fitting. **P** - Thetford **CM**

AS163
Gilt-bronze mount. **CM**

A very fine interlacing pattern is evident on the gilt-bronze rectangular chip-carved mount shown as **AS163**, which again dates from the mid 8th century. This may have been part of a horse harness strap decoration.

An earlier openwork disc mount dating from the early 7th century is shown as **AS164**. It has a fish in the centre with two pairs of fins on each side. The outer border is decorated with crescents, triangles and leaf shapes, while at the base on each side is a triple-banded snake-like creature of Style II Animal design. The fish design could have a Christian significance or indeed a mythological symbolism.

reused as a pendant in antiquity. The style of art of the late 8th century is very distinctive and quite detailed but is also the rarest.

AS161 is a very elegant gilt-bronze chip-carved rectangular shaped fitting. It shows a quadruped with an interlaced pattern enclosing the body. It again dates from the late 8th century.

AS162 is a wolf-like terminal made of gilded bronze with chip-carved detailing and two circular glass eyes. There is an interlacing double-banded decoration on the body, which gives it an 8th century date. It may have formed one arm of a cross from the lid of a reliquary shrine.

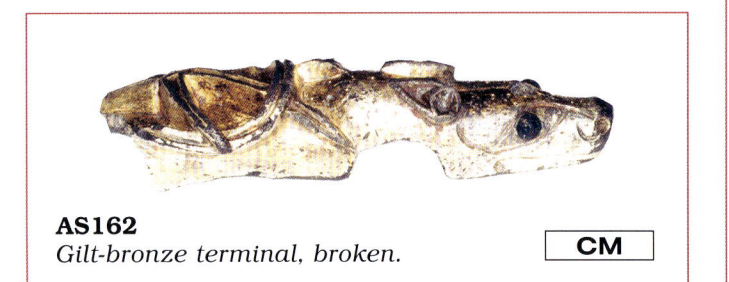

AS162
Gilt-bronze terminal, broken. **CM**

AS164
Gilt-bronze openwork mount. **P** - Kent **CM**

A later Anglo-Scandinavian bronze circular mount dating from the 10th century is shown as **V165** It has an engraved design depicting two outward-facing birds (either eagles or ravens) with an outer border of leaf-shaped ornamentation. The birds could be representations of Hugin and Munin, who informed Odin of important news.

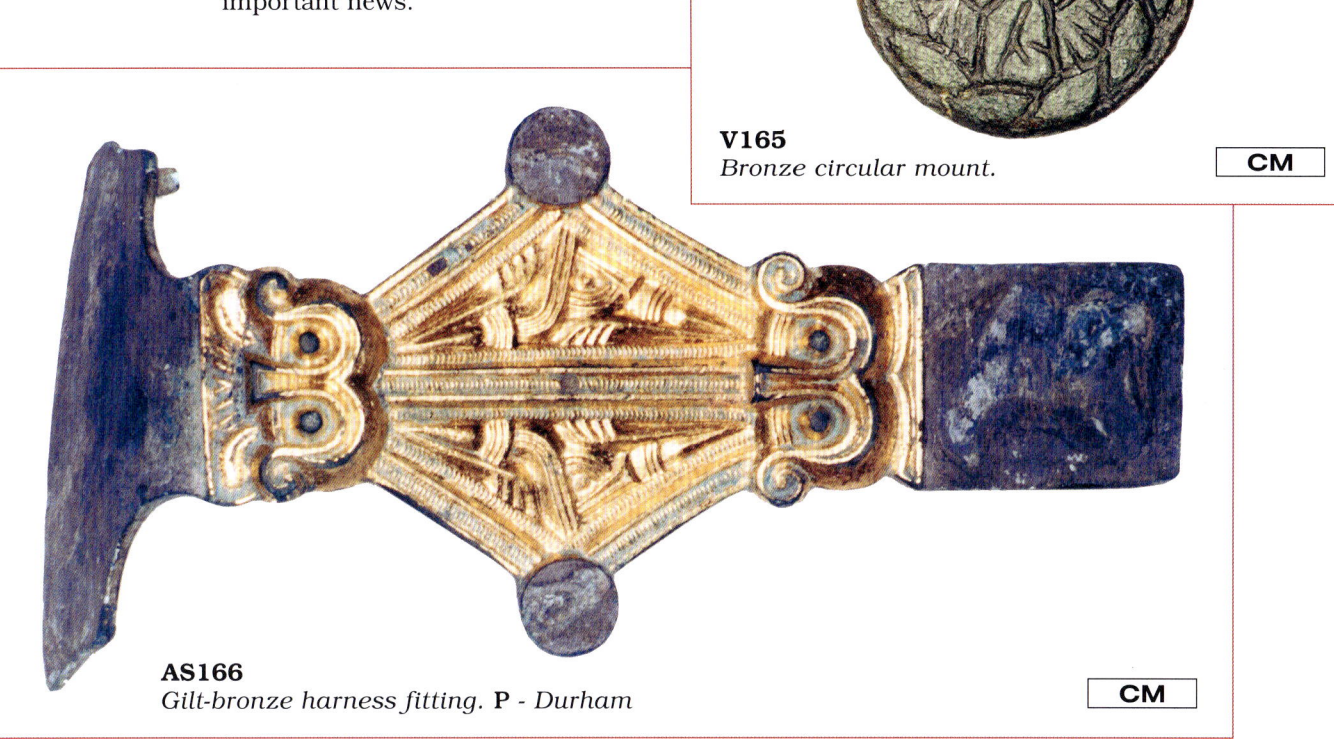

V165
Bronze circular mount.

AS166
Gilt-bronze harness fitting. **P** - *Durham*

A very specific mount, dating from the 6th century is shown as **AS166**. This may have been part of a scabbard or harness fitting. The lozenge-shaped centre is divided into two panels with Style I Animal decoration. The beast has a triple-stranded ribbon-like body with a crouching leg motif and three claws. The central dividing line and outer border are decorated with bands of fine punches. At the top and base are two facemasks with arched eyebrows with scroll ends and two circular eyes. The gilding is almost fully intact, which reveals the fine quality

V167
Gilt-bronze openwork box mount.

of the design. The end plates were probably decorated with repousse silver panels, but are now missing.

A possible box mount is shown as **V167**. It is of gilt-bronze with an openwork design of interlaced pattern in Borre style. It dates from the late 9th century and has fixing holes equally spaced around its perimeter.

Another Viking bronze mount of Ringerike style is shown as **V168**. It shows a beast with interlacing and openwork design. It dates from the early 11th century.

A very late Viking bronze mount is shown as **V169**. It is of Urnes style and dates from the mid 11th century. It is of openwork form with two beasts with snake-like bodies.

Norse mythology is rarely represented but **V170** appears to show Odin being consumed by the wolf Fenrir at the battle of Ragnarok. The wolf's head encloses the body of Odin who has his arms around the wolf's claws. The figure is crudely detailed. It may be a mount or a terminal, and dates from the 10th century.

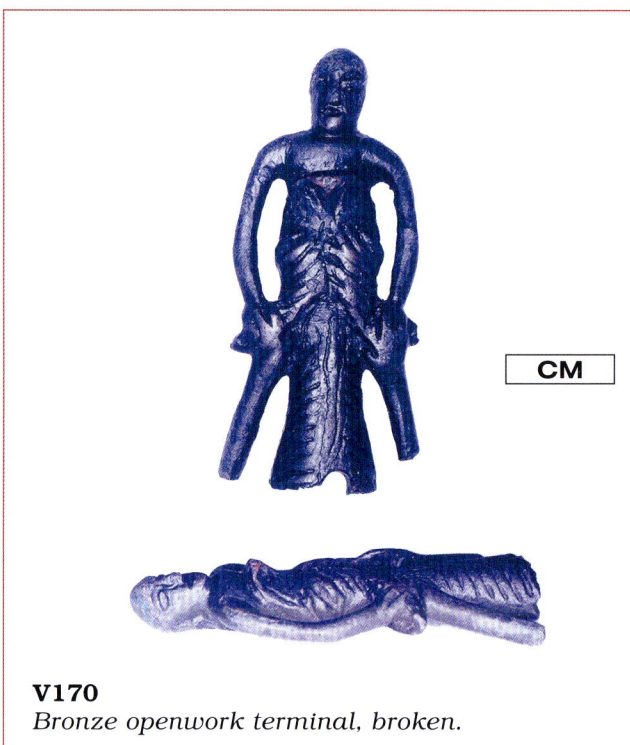

V168
Bronze mount, Ringerike style.

V169
Bronze mount, Urnes style.

V170
Bronze openwork terminal, broken.

Price Guide

		Fine	Very Fine			Fine	Very Fine
AS130	Bronze girdle hanger.	£60	£140	**AS150**	Bronze triangular mount.	£55	£140
AS131	Bronze key with lozenge bow.	£40	£90	**AS151**	Bronze triangular mount.	£60	£160
AS132	Bronze key with openwork bow.	£75	£200	**AS152**	Gilt bronze disc mount.	£70	£200
AS133	Bronze key with openwork bow.	£65	£175	**AS153**	Gilded disc mount with garnets.	£140	£350
AS134	Large bronze key with cut-out bow.	£100	£275	**AS154**	Chip-carved bronze die.	£120	£280
AS135	Bronze key with annular bow.	£50	£120	**AS155**	Silver-gilt facemask.	£130	£300
V136	Key with decorated brass shank.	£175	£450	**AS156**	Gilt-bronze facemask.	£35	£90
V137	Iron key inlaid with brass decoration.	£35	£120	**AS157**	Small triangular bronze mount.	£40	£110
AS138	Bronze spoon.	£180	£450	**AS158**	Bronze harness mount.	£85	£240
AS139	Bronze hanging bowl mount.	£45	£125	**AS159**	Gilt-bronze mount.	£475	£1,400
AS140	Bronze hanging bowl mount.	£40	£110	**AS160**	Gilt-bronze mount.	£375	£1,100
AS141	Bronze hanging bowl mount.	£35	£85	**AS161**	Gilt-bronze fitting.	£140	£350
AS142	Bronze hanging bowl mount.	£30	£75	**AS162**	Gilt-bronze terminal, broken.	£110	£250
AS143	Bronze trefoil bucket mount.	£55	£170	**AS163**	Gilt-bronze mount.	£100	£220
AS144	Bronze bucket frame.	£25	£60	**AS164**	Gilt-bronze openwork mount.	£175	£450
AS145	Bronze rectangular mount.	£65	£180	**V165**	Bronze circular mount.	£70	£175
AS146	Bronze circular mount.	£75	£220	**AS166**	Gilt-bronze harness fitting.	£220	£550
AS147	Bronze circular mount.	£300	£800	**V167**	Gilt-bronze openwork box mount.	£450	£1,200
AS148	Gilt-bronze rectangular mount.	£70	£200	**V168**	Bronze mount, Ringerike style.	£90	£260
AS149	Gilt-bronze circular mount.	£65	£180	**V169**	Bronze mount, Urnes style.	£85	£250
				V170	Bronze openwork terminal, broken.	£220	£500

Chapter 7

Jewellery & Beads

Pendants

During the late 5th century, and throughout the 6th century, Roman coins (and subsequently Merovingian coins) were worn by Saxon women as amuletic jewellery. Such coins were mounted in beaded gold wire frames, to which was attached a corrugated or ribbed suspension loop. Circular pendants of gold foil, based on the portraits of late Roman emperors that had appeared on coins, were also popular in Scandinavia from the 5th century right through to the 8th century, and developed their own distinctive style with a stamped repousse design.

M193
Gold bracteate pendant. CM

M193 is an example of a very barbarous portrait, facing right, with abstract designs in front of the face. Because it is repousse the design is incuse on the reverse. The pendant has a raised beaded rim and the suspension loop has three ribs, the central one being the largest. This is a normal feature for pendants of this period.

A number of gold Merovingian thrymsas found in England show evidence of having being mounted as pendants, or even having been pierced for suspension. The majority are found in south-east Britain, with their distribution also extending along the east coast.

Jewelled pendants, also predominantly recovered from Kent, were worn by women during the late 6th to the late 7th centuries. These were made of gold and are generally circular in shape, but occasionally examples are found that are cruciform in outline or - even rarer - of crescent shape. Most have an imitative form of filigree decoration. **AS194** is a very fine example of Kentish form, which is larger than normal in size. In the centre is a domed setting of white material (possibly shell) with a cabochon garnet set into the apex, which is framed with a ribbed collar. Around this are three concentric bands of pseudo-plaitwork imitating filigree. The inner ring contains annulets, arranged mainly in pairs. The middle band has gold wire C-scrolls, while the outer band has annulets with an S-scroll at the top below the ribbed suspension loop, which is tubular in section. Unfortunately, the lower part of the disc has been broken, probably due to plough damage, and the gold is too thin and fragile to be repaired. This example is likely to date from the mid 7th century as silver has been added to the gold making it a paler colour.

Another gold disc pendant, shown as **AS195**, is of much simpler form and more representative of the average size. In the centre is a flat circular garnet enclosed within a central raised circular cell with two collars of gold wire, one ribbed and one plain.

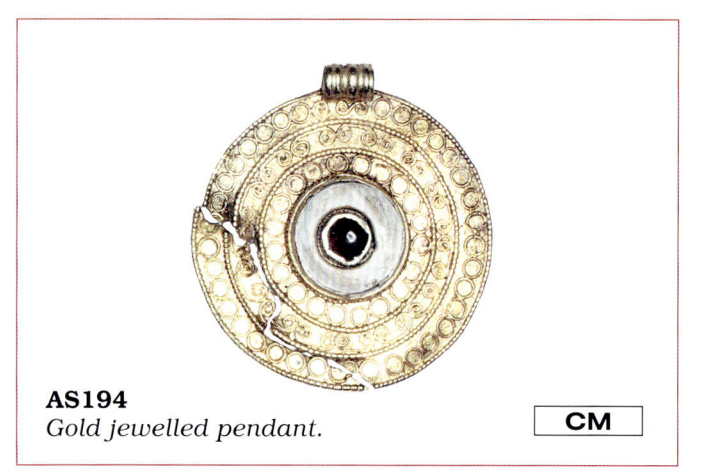

AS194
Gold jewelled pendant. CM

AS195
Gold jewelled pendant. CM

The decoration is minimal, consisting of four straight bands of plain wire enclosed within fine beaded wire strips forming a cross pattern with crescent-shaped terminals. Around the rim there is a band of plain wire. The suspension loop at the top is of thin corrugated gold. The likely date for this piece is early 7th century with the cross design indicating an early Christian influence.

Many of the known Saxon gold pendants consist of cloisonné work set with garnets. Pre-cut garnets were readily available from the Continent during the 6th and early 7th centuries. They were reused and re-cut during the middle of the 7th century (sometimes quite badly) when the supply diminished. One distinctive feature of garnet cutting at this time is that the stones do not have a curved surface (cabochon), but rather have been cut into small thin flat sections, which were then polished. This was achieved by splitting the garnets along their natural planes, a quite easy task because of the poor quality of the garnets being used. To maximise the intensity of the colour of the garnet, die-stamped wafer thin gold foil was inserted beneath each stone to reflect light. Each foil was stamped with crosshatched lines, sometimes arranged in boxed patterns. The lines are extremely small, varying from one to five per millimetre. This is almost on a microscopic scale, and was a considerable achievement taking into consideration the simple tools available at the time.

AS197
Gold drop pendant with garnet.
CM

Another important and distinctive gold pendant that dates from the mid 7th century takes the form known as cabochon or "drop" pendant. The known examples have been found predominantly in the south-east of England. **AS197** is a very fine example with a large elongated and oval (tear-shaped) cabochon garnet in a gem setting. It is surrounded by three collars of beaded wire, the central band being of heavier gauge than the others. The suspension loop at the top has three ribs. Most of these pendants have oval garnets, but occasionally amethyst or glass was used as a central setting. On a Saxon necklace that was found in the 19th century, several of these drop pendants had been used, alternated with gold discs.

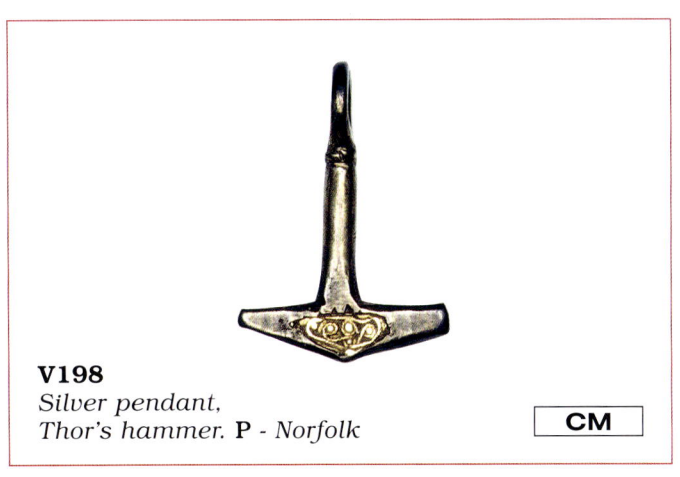

AS196
Gold disc brooch (?).
CM

V198
Silver pendant, Thor's hammer. P - Norfolk
CM

AS196 is an interesting gold disc formed from eight twisted bands of wire soldered together with an outer border of coils. There is a large opening in the centre, which may have contained a coin or decorative disc. There is also an opening on both sides, for suspension or for a pin. This could have been used as a brooch or as a decoration suspended from a necklace. It would date 7th or 8th century.

After the Viking invasion amuletic pendants representing Thor's hammer were worn in Britain especially in the north. **V198** is an example in silver cut from sheet metal with a suspension loop at the butt of the shaft. In the centre of the hammerhead is a triangular recess that has a gold filigree insert that has probably been taken from another piece of jewellery. The hammerhead itself can be boat shaped or rectangular. This example dates from the 10th century.

Rings

During the 5th and 6th centuries simple finger rings (in silver or bronze) were worn by women on the left hand. These rings usually consisted of a spiral band, having rounded terminals that could be either flat or rounded in section. Some examples show grooved punches as decoration.

During the 6th and 7th centuries, a bezel formed from twisted wire into a flat spiral became popular as a design. Such rings were usually made of bronze, but occasionally were formed from silver. A distinctive feature of these rings was that the ends of the spiral were wound around on each side of the bezel. The same design continued in use into the Viking period.

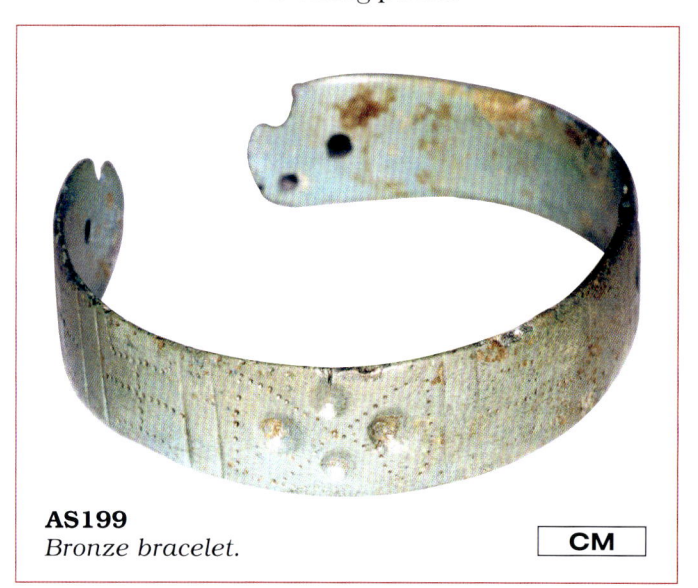

AS199
Bronze bracelet.

During the 5th and 6th centuries bronze bracelets were mainly worn by children. One example, shown as **AS199** is of sheet metal that is flat in section, and is of penannular shape. It is decorated with pairs of incised transverse lines - separating rectangular panels - which have patterns of small punched dots arranged around four symmetrical large circular punches. On the terminals of the bracelet are additional fixing holes.

It is very difficult to precisely date Anglo-Saxon rings, and to differentiate them from some of the simple later Viking types - particularly if there is no decoration or the pattern consists simply of spirals of wire. **AS200** is a band of tapering form made from strips of gold wire hammered and soldered together. In the centre is a band of spirals of flattened coiled gold wire with two outer bands of plain wire on each side. The ring has been cut at the back, either for removal or for resizing. A suggested date would be 8th or 9th century.

AS201
Large gold filigree ring, oval bezel.

In the late 8th century through to the 9th century, rings developed large oval bezels that sloped at the shoulders. Each known example has its own distinctive form of decoration. Some have an interlacing quadruped with a speckled body, while others have a bust and an inscription relating to the owner or allegiance to a king. **AS201** is a spectacular filigree gold ring with an enormous oval bezel. Set into the centre is a very corroded red stone (either glass or a garnet). Around this are concentric bands of braided wire. The hoop of the ring is tapered and decorated in a similar style. Additionally, on the shoulders are three circular beads arranged in a trefoil pattern. Unfortunately, the ring is badly cracked around its hoop but clearly shows the flamboyance of jewellery of this period.

Another gold-banded finger ring is **AS202**. This has two separate bands of gold pleated wire separated by two plain bands, and a plain band

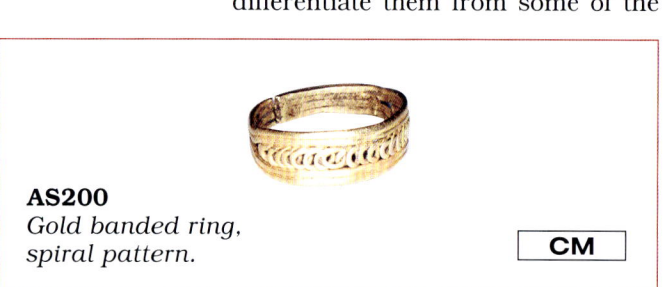

AS200
Gold banded ring, spiral pattern.

AS202
Gold ring of pleated wire.

on each edge. At the back of the hoop the ring tapers slightly, and the bands of wire have been hammered together to form a flat surface. This example is likely to be 8th or 9th century in date. Unfortunately, it had been damaged in the ground and has received careful restoration.

During the 9th century there were several recognised forms of rings. In the early 9th century Trewhiddle style design was used to ornament the expanded bezel, while in the late 9th century, in the north of Britain, a circular bezel was decorated with a spotted beast. Banded gold rings, bearing an inscription on the outside also occur. **AS203** is a bronze band with an incised inscription running around the whole of the outside. Some of the letters appear runic in form and have notched sides. This ring is possibly 9th century in date.

AS203
Bronze ring with inscription. `CM`

One of the most famous 9th century gold artefacts known is the gold aestal or pointer with King Alfred's name appearing on it. It is recorded that he sent one of these to every bishop in the kingdom. Each had a value of 50 mancuses.

A few rings bear Christian devices alongside pagan symbols. One example has the lettering and symbol representing *Agnus Dei* (or Pascal Lamb) on the bezel.

A few Saxon rings were set with re-used Roman intaglios. Some of these rings are Merovingian in origin.

In the Viking period, kings gave rings to their supporters to maintain allegiance. These rings are usually of gold or silver and could be traded as hack-silver.

V204
Bronze decorated ring with coiled ends. `CM`

Most of the Viking rings have the hoop ends coiled around themselves, acting as a knot. **V204** is a bronze ring with a wide bezel of flattened form with ring and dot punches stamped along its length. The back of the hoop consists of a narrow band of circular section, with its ends curled around each other. This is typical style of the 9th and 10th century period.

V205
Silver ring with coiled ends. `CM`

The silver ring, shown as **V205**, is of simpler form with a spiral of square section silver; again each end curls around the other. On this example, the device could represent the decoration for the front of the ring.

V206
Gold ring with multi-coiled ends. `CM`

A gold example is shown in **V206**. This is a single rounded band, with its ends curled around eight times on one side and six on the other acting as a form of security and as decoration. This example would date 9th-10th century.

A lot of Viking jewellery has a punched decoration. **V207** is a silver ring dating from the 10th century with an expanded lozenge shape bezel and a central boss. Around this

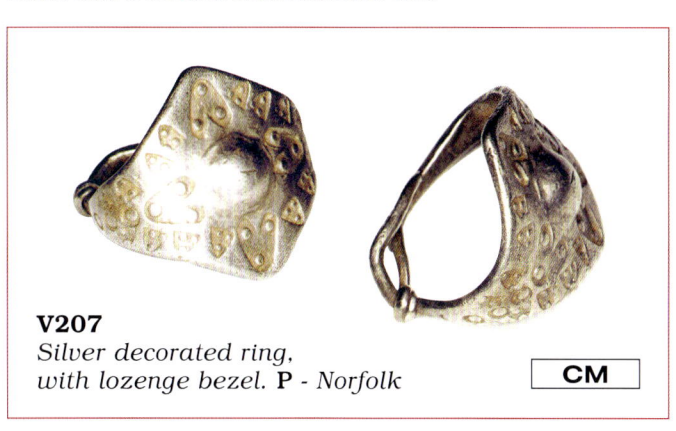

V207
Silver decorated ring, with lozenge bezel. **P** - *Norfolk* `CM`

are a series of triangular and heart-shaped punches, each with three pellets one in each corner. The hoop of the ring tapers sharply and is of thin flat section with the ends curled around each other (although on this example one end has suffered damage in antiquity).

V208
Silver ring with niello inlay. CM

Another form of decoration used at this time was niello inlay. **V208** is a flat band with square panels inlaid with niello forming cross motifs within squares. The ring is penannular in form, although this may have resulted from plough damage. I would suggest an 11th century date for this item.

A number of Viking silver arm rings are of penannular form, and these have been found in hoards of hack silver (both complete and cut up into sections).

The bronze ring shown as **AS209** is flat in section and of uniform thickness. It has a punched design forming straight-sided Ss running around the centre panel. The top of the ring is indicated by two rows of three horizontal Ss. I would suggest a 9th century date.

AS209
Bronze ring with punched decoration. CM

Beads

In the 5th and 6th centuries Saxon women wore strings of beads suspended between pairs of brooches fixed at their shoulders. However, a few exceptionally large beads have been found in male graves dating to the period. In addition, women wore long necklaces adorned with coins and toilet implement alongside decorative beads. A total of 104 beads have been excavated from a single female grave.

AS210
Blue glass bead, undamaged. **P** - *S Humberside* CM

The most common form of bead consists of monochrome glass. **AS210** shows three thin annular dark blue translucent beads of similar form. These are the most common colour and shape of glass bead that were used in Britain. The second most common form of glass bead is shown

AS211
Red glass bead, undamaged. **P** - *S Humberside* CM

as **AS211**, which is bun-shaped with a rust-red colour. Saxon beads are known in a variety of shapes and colours. They can be barrel-shaped, cylindrical, polyhedral, biconical, melon, segmented, or bi-convex in form as well as the above. The colours used individually and in combination include yellow, blue, green blue, white calcite, black, and brown.

AS212 is a globular rust-red bead with a wave or spiral pattern of green and yellow bands.

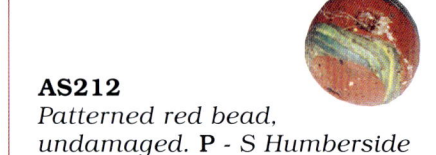

AS212
Patterned red bead, undamaged. **P** - *S Humberside* CM

AS213
Large patterned multi-coloured bead, undamaged. **P** - *S Humberside*

CM

AS214
Amber bead, crude form. **P** - *S Humberside*

CM

AS213 is a larger globular bead with crossed waves of red and blue on a white core.

Beads were also made from amber. **AS214** is an example of rough disc form; Saxon amber beads are usually irregular in shape. Such beads were widely worn in the late 6th and 7th centuries and were regarded as more valuable than the glass counterparts. Additionally, rock crystal was used for beads in the 5th and 6th centuries and occasionally amethyst was used in the 7th century. Most of the beads, including the glass examples, were imported.

Metal beads were also used. At first they were made of bronze, but in the late 6th and 7th centuries bi-conical gold beads with braided wire came into fashion with the increased availability of gold.

Price Guide

		Fine	Very Fine			Fine	Very Fine
M193	Gold bracteate pendant.	£750	£1,800	**V204**	Bronze decorated ring with coiled ends.	£80	£220
AS194	Gold jewelled pendant.	£2,400	£6,000	**V205**	Silver ring with coiled ends.	£60	£130
AS195	Gold jewelled pendant.	£900	£2,200	**V206**	Gold ring with multi-coiled ends.	£200	£500
AS196	Gold disc brooch (?).	£125	£275	**V207**	Silver decorated ring, with lozenge bezel.	£220	£550
AS197	Gold drop pendant with garnet.	£550	£1,300	**V208**	Silver ring with niello inlay.	£130	£350
V198	Silver pendant, Thor's hammer.	£150	£375	**AS209**	Bronze ring with punched decoration.	£50	£125
AS199	Bronze bracelet.	£85	£230	**AS210**	Blue glass bead, undamaged.		£10
AS200	Gold banded ring, spiral pattern.	£550	£1,400	**AS211**	Red glass bead, undamaged.		£10
AS201	Large gold filigree ring, oval bezel.	£4,800	£13,000	**AS212**	Patterned red bead, undamaged.		£18
AS202	Gold ring of pleated wire.	£450	£1,100	**AS213**	Large patterned multi-coloured bead, undamaged.		£25
AS203	Bronze ring with inscription.	£160	£450	**AS214**	Amber bead, crude form.		£8-£10.

Chapter 8

Stirrup Mounts & Harness Fittings

Over the last ten years a number of artefacts have been re-identified. This is partially a result of the greater numbers that have been found by individual detectorists, but also because of the general increased interest in, and awareness of, our past. One example of this is a series of 11th century Viking-inspired stirrup mounts.

The stirrup itself was unknown to the Ancient World, and was introduced into England quite late in our history by the Vikings. The word itself derives from the Anglo-Saxon *stigan* to mount and *rap* a rope. The earliest Scandinavian example known comes from a 9th century grave excavated in Norway. The earliest depiction of stirrups in use in England appears on the Bayeux Tapestry.

A book published in 1997 by David Williams established that a series of so-called book mounts were in fact fittings that connected the leather strap to the iron stirrup. When comparison was made to Scandinavian examples of stirrup mounts found in graves in Sweden, a close similarity in style and form was observed to the English "book mounts". Although the Scandinavian mounts were larger than the English examples, the purpose was the same.

The two main shapes found in England are triangular and rectangular (trapezoidal). All have a flange at the wider or lower edge, all are of robust design, all are cast in bronze (or sometimes in copper), and all have a decorated front side. In use they were positioned vertically with the mount's lower flange sited underneath the top edge of the triangular shaped iron stirrup (see diagram). There are usually two lower iron rivets with an additional rivet at the top, and these are connected to a vertical backing bar of iron. The leather strap for the stirrup fitted between the mount and the stirrup. In this way, the backing bar also acted as a reinforcement to the leather. The particular English form is an Anglo-Scandinavian version of the original 10th century Scandinavian prototypes.

It would appear from the 600 or more examples that have been found - as individual losses from all over England - that stirrup mounts were not suitable for prolonged use. The weight and method of attachment is likely to have worn away the leather strap, hence the considerable numbers that have been found.

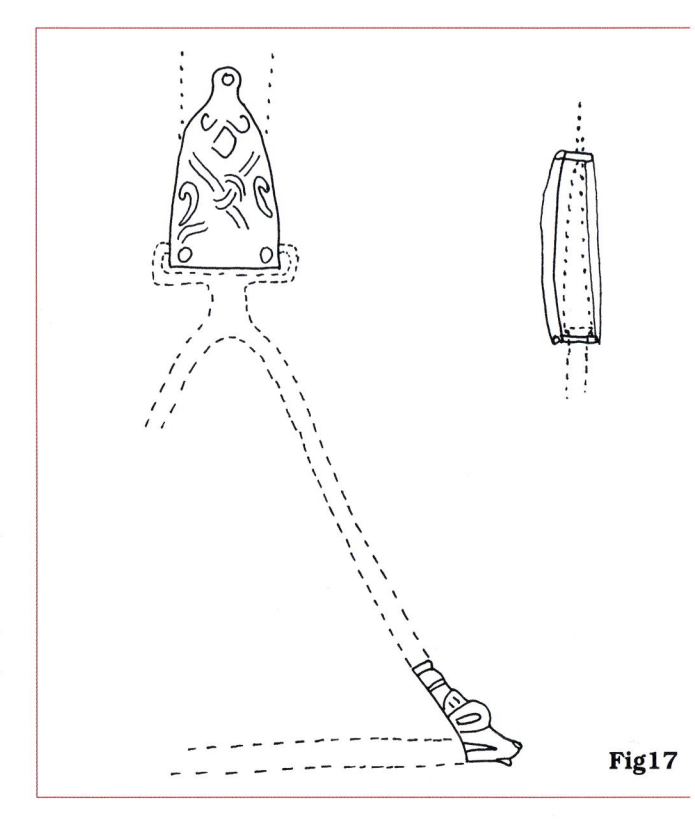

An example of a stirrup terminal, which is in copper and decorated with an animal's head is shown as **V220**. This has a hollow underside to receive the lower edge of the iron stirrup. There would have been one of these fittings on each side, and sometimes smaller ones at the top edges. Several examples have been found with part of the iron stirrup still in place. The detailing is of quite high relief with raised oval eyes, projecting snout, and a tusk at each

Fig17

V220
Copper stirrup terminal.

side. It may represent a dragon but this design is generally referred to as a "beast" as it has elements of a horse, wolf, and boar within its iconography.

There is quite a range of different shapes and styles of decoration on these stirrup mounts and the following examples represent the most common forms.

V221
Triangular stirrup mount of abstract Ringerike design.

CM

V222 is an example that has an engraved abstract Ringerike design based on two heads (one on each side) linked together by a knot around the body. On this example the link is a simple horizontal line. Because of the degradation of style, this mount is likely to be of mid 11th century date. The early type has a much more intricate design with the ribbon-like bodies interconnecting.

V222
Triangular stirrup mount, two dragons design.

CM

The mount shown as **V222** has a zoomorphic terminal at the top, which is slightly damaged on this example. There are two dragons' heads at the lower end with the ribbon-like bodies framing the edge. This again would be of mid 11th century date.

Some of the most elaborate mounts are very striking and perhaps show elements of Norse mythology in their representations. **V223** is a magnificent example and must have come from the horse accoutrements of an important Viking warrior. It shows a naked man standing with his legs bound with snakes, and with a wolf across his back and in front of his arms. There is also a snake tied around his waist with its head hanging down between the man's legs. The man has a moustache and beard with the ribs shown as three pairs of curving lines. His nipples and navel are also shown. The snakes that form the

V223
Triangular stirrup mount, figure bound with snakes.
P - *Norfolk*

CM

framework were originally inlaid with niello and silver panels, but only a few traces of this remain. There have been just over 10 examples of this type found in England. Most are of a more degraded or abstract form, so this example is likely to be a prototype and I would suggest an early 11th century date.

One interpretation of this iconography is that it represents the god Loki who was being pursued by the other gods for the murder of Balder. They imprisoned Loki in a cave and tie him with the gut of his son Narvi around his hips and his legs. (Loki's other son Vali was turned into a wolf who then sunk his teeth into Narvi, killing him). In this state Loki was held until Ragnarok, which symbolised the end of the world. While he was bound the world would continue. It was perceived that an earthquake represented the writhing of Loki from having serpent venom splashed on his face while he was bound.

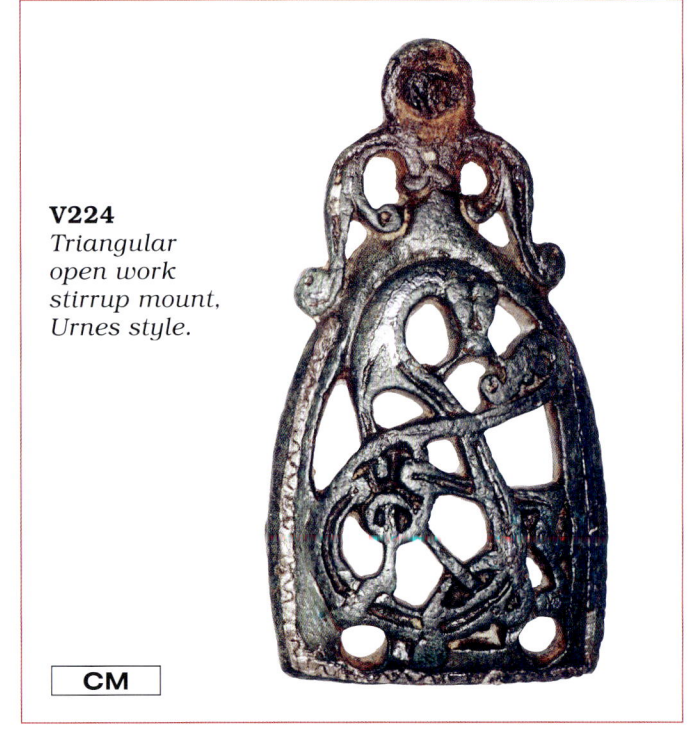

V225
Rectangular stirrup mount, human mask.

CM

V224
Triangular open work stirrup mount, Urnes style.

CM

design is reminiscent of the Wodan head used on Frisian sceats in the 8th century. This mount probably dates from the mid 11th century.

Another mount of rectangular form, **V226**, has a raised animal's head with pierced circular eyes. The edges of the mount are scalloped, and this is now regarded as an East Anglian form. It dates mid 11th century.

V226
Rectangular stirrup mount, animal mask.

CM

Another spectacular mount is **V224**, which is of open work design containing ribbon bodied dragons with interlacing and knotted bodies. This is in the Urnes style dating from the mid 11th century. There is a border of silver with a zigzag line engraved into it. At the top are tendrils extending from the central rivet. The use of floral decoration, especially tendrils with curled over ends, is common on many Viking objects of the 11th century. There is a series of stirrup mounts utilising floral decoration as a main theme, and this could indicate a tree that in Norse mythology was called Yggdrasill (an ash tree).

Other pictorial mounts show various styles of heads, both human and animal. **V225** is a much smaller square-shaped mount in bronze with a human mask. It has an engraved design, which on this example is slightly cruder than usual. The face has a projecting chin with square sides and rectangular-shaped eyes; the grooves at the sides of the face may indicate a moustache. This

One of the most common mounts, **AS227**, is of triangular form showing an upward looking lion with its mouth open. One front leg is raised, while the tail curls between the back legs. For many years this type was mistakenly believed to be a form of heraldic pendant of the 13th or 14th century. It is a very common type with little variation other than the way in which the animal is facing. Perhaps this is an example dating from after the Norman Conquest when a more standardised design would have been adopted. This would indicate a late 11th century date.

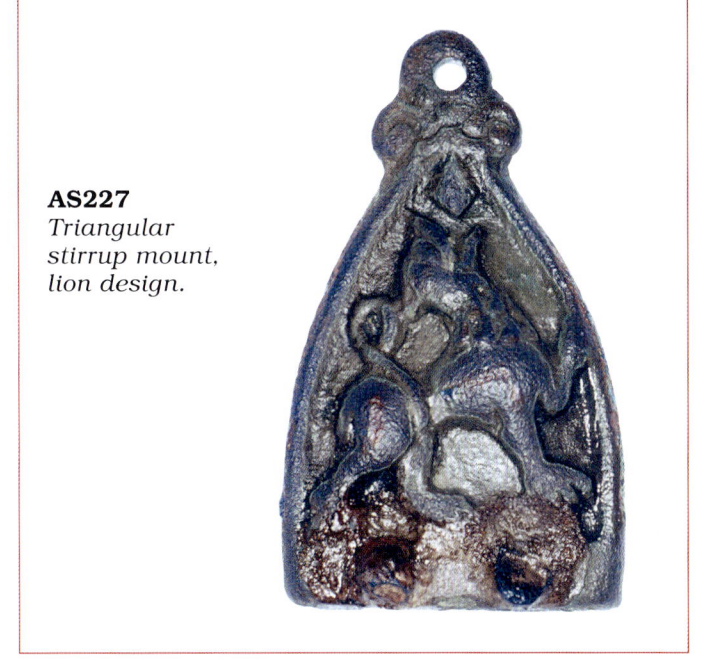

AS227
Triangular stirrup mount, lion design.

V229
Triangular stirrup mount, two animal heads.

The simplest and most basic of all the stirrup mounts, **AS228**, has a lozenge shape with an open work cross design with three circular knobs across the centre. It has punched triangles in two lines continuing all the way around the surface. The use of a cross design may indicate a Christian and Norman influence, and this again would suggest a late 11th century date.

V230
Rectangular stirrup mount, animal's head.

AS228
Lozenge stirrup mount, cross design.

V231
Triangular stirrup mount, interlaced pattern.

The last two designs, because of their standardisation, suggest widespread usage. A number of variations of the designs used on stirrup mounts include those with quite a large-eared animal. **V229** has two heads, mounted one above the other. The top one has a pointed nose and large oval-shaped ears resembling a

81

V232
Viking strap mount, interlaced pattern.
P - Lincolnshire

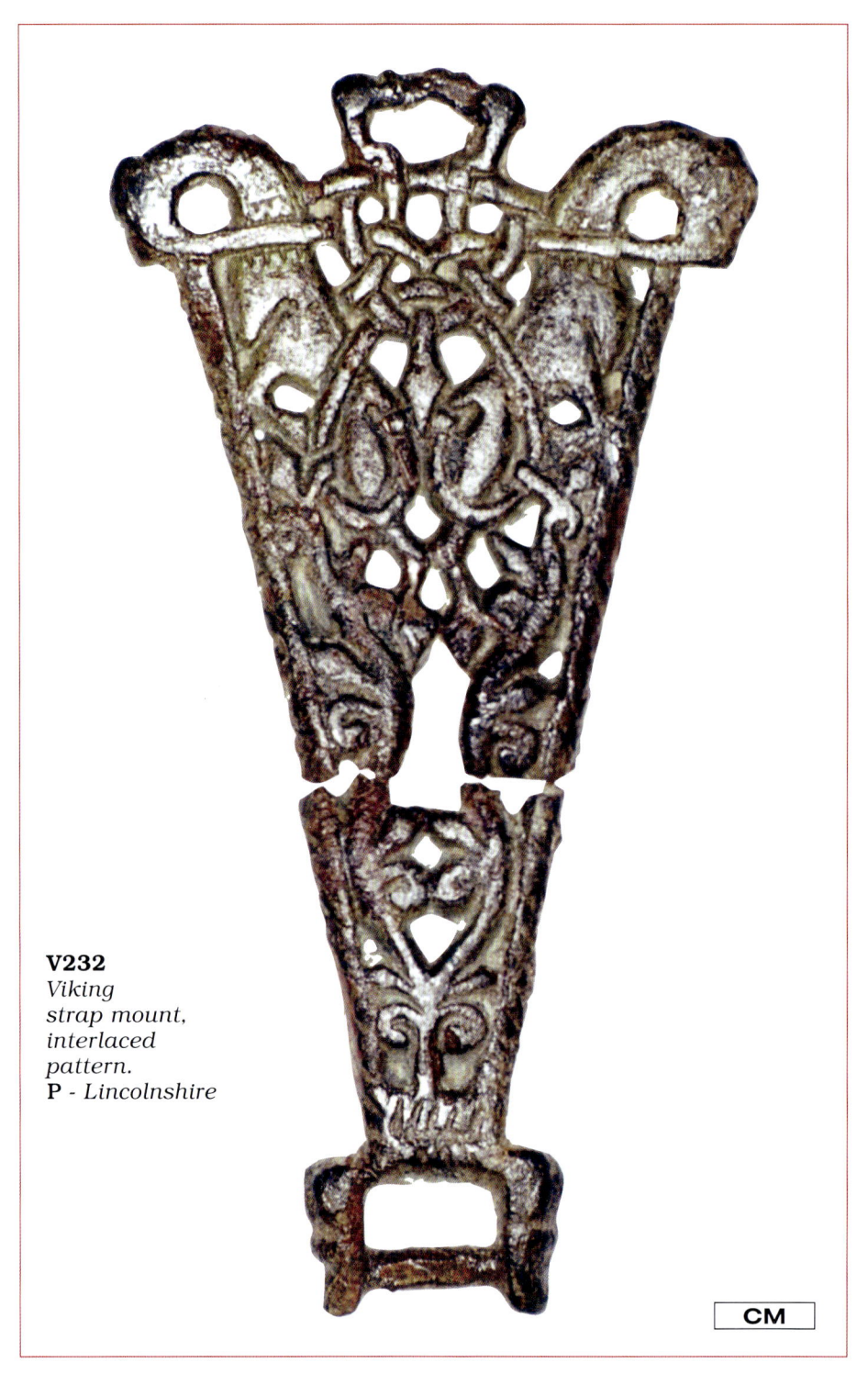

mouse or a bat. The lower animal has circular eyes and again extended ears. There are tendrils around the two rivet holes at the base.

A variation using a similar animal's head is shown as **V230**. This one is of rectangular form with four pairs of apertures. There are many variations of this type, some of which have engraved decoration around the central head. Many of the examples that have been found show clear evidence of wear, particularly around the edges. Sometimes this also causes the central design to wear smooth.

The last example of stirrup mount is of triangular form and shown as **V231**. It has an interlacing ribbon pattern with an animal's head at the top.

Other examples of horse furniture are rare, especially from the Viking period. **V232** is a large triangular shaped bronze fitting, too large to be a stirrup mount. It was perhaps used for a saddle or harness strap. The surface is decorated with interlacing and ribbon-like beasts with knots around the bodies. At the base there are tendrils from which the animals emerge. There are two rivet holes at

V233
Viking cheek piece.

the top with a rectangular connecting bar between, and there is a more pronounced rectangular connecting bar at the bottom with animals' heads on each side. It has been ritually broken across the centre, rendering it unusable. It would date from the 11th century.

Parts of the horse bridle in bronze or copper from the Viking period are more commonly found. **V233** is part of a cheek piece with an animal's head with a curving body and open jaws that form one of the loops. The simple engraved features quickly wear down and are often indistinguishable. This example also has knobs as additional decoration. This piece would date to the early 11th century.

Price Guide

		Fine	Very Fine			Fine	Very Fine
V220	Copper stirrup terminal	£12	£26	**AS227**	Triangular stirrup mount, lion design.	£30	£80
V221	Triangular stirrup mount of abstract design.	£25	£55	**AS228**	Lozenge stirrup mount, cross design.	£18	£40
V222	Triangular stirrup mount, two dragons design.	£22	£50	**V229**	Triangular stirrup mount, two animal heads.	£50	£130
V223	Triangular stirrup mount, figure bound with snakes.	£300	£750	**V230**	Rectangular stirrup mount, animal's head.	£30	£70
V224	Triangular open work stirrup mount, Urnes style.	£350	£850	**V231**	Triangular stirrup mount, interlaced pattern.	£32 VF	£90
V225	Rectangular stirrup mount, human mask.	£45	£120	**V232**	Viking strap mount, interlaced pattern.	£600	£1500
V226	Rectangular stirrup mount, animal mask.	£30	£85	**V233**	Viking bridle fitting.	£45	£140

Chapter 9

Weights & Gaming Counters

Little is known about the use of weights and scales during the Anglo-Saxon period. From excavations, however, it appears that the Saxons used worn bronze Roman coins as weights by marking them with a series of punches, usually annulets or ring and dot. The system of measures would have been based on the gold *thrymsa* or *tremisses* (weighing 1.3gm) first struck in Britain around AD 620. Merovingian prototypes for these coins came from Germany and France, and were introduced to Britain in the late 6th century. During the 7th century the gold gradually became mixed with silver creating a pale yellow colour (electrum). In around AD 675 the gold used for these coins was entirely replaced by silver.

From AD 700 the system of weights was based on Arabic coins called *dinars* and *dirhams*. The gold *dinar* weighed 4.23gm and was called a *mancus* by the Anglo-Saxons. The silver *dirham* weighed 2.97gm, and the bullion *dirham* weighed 3.13gm. By the 11th century AD a *mancus* referred to 30 silver pennies, while 8 *mancus* made a pound or 240 pence.

An example of a bronze weight or steelyard poise that probably dates from the 7th or 8th century is shown as **AS234**. It is a solid cube with four of the sides decorated with facemasks. Each of the faces has lentoid eyes. The eyes of three of the masks are set with blue glass beads, while the fourth has no pupils and this may represent that the eyes are closed. The nose on each mask is long and wedge shaped, while the mouth is depicted as a straight slit. At the top of the mask the hair is shown either as vertical grooves or horizontal waves. The four faces could represent a Saxon interpretation of a Janus head. At the top of the weight are the remains of an integrally cast bronze suspension loop. The weight is 10.2gm and presumably it would have been suspended on a chain from the arm of a balance.

Throughout the Viking period items of precious metal were chopped up into small pieces, which are referred to as "hacked" or "hack" silver or gold. These roughly cut pieces would have served as currency. The Vikings had no coinage of their own and used other countries' looted treasures to facilitate trading.

V235
Bronze plated iron sphere weight or 3 ortugar 23.7gms.

CM

The Vikings used a system of weights based on the *ortugar*. These are normally flattened spheres made of iron and cased in bronze (see **V235**) and were based on late Roman examples. They were used primarily for weighing silver. Five found together in a male grave in Sweden could represent a set. Except for the smallest, each is marked by a series of circles (1, 3, 4, and 5). They weigh 3.99gm (half an *ortugar*), 8.22gm (1 *ortugar*), 22.92gm (3 *ortugar*), 31.37 (4 *ortugar*), and 39.32gm (5 *ortugar*). (Eight *ore* equals 24 *ortugar*). The top and base of these weights are decorated with dotted rings and the mark of value.

The other type of weight used in Viking times is a bronze polyhedral an example being shown as **V236**. These are quite small and have dots

AS234
Bronze cube weight decorated with facemasks. **P - S Derbyshire**

on each side indicating the value. These are 1, 2, 3, 4, and 6. The denomination of a unit has been calculated at 0.65gm, but there is some variation in the examples that I have weighed. Two examples of the 2 dot weighed 0.8gm and 1.1gm; the 3 dot illustrated weighs 1.5gm (instead of 1.95gm); two 4 dot examples weighed 2.4gm and 2.6gm (the latter being the correct weight); while examples of the 6 dot weighed between 3.7gm and 4 gm (the correct weight is 3.9gm). The smallest example, the 1 dot, is quite rare probably because it is so difficult to find. These weights were primarily used for weighing hack gold, and are found in the Viking occupied areas of England. The largest type, the 6 dot, is almost the weight of a gold *dinar*.

V236
Polyhedral bronze weight.

CM

Enlarged

In AD 973 there was a major reform of the coinage in England with the silver penny now weighing between 1.1gm and 1.8gm.

Some curious lead weights, inset with chip carved fragments or even coins, have also been found on a number of Viking sites in the north of England and Ireland. These have been tentatively dated from the coins to c830-874. A number of these have been found in a site in Lincolnshire.

V237 is a solid triangular shaped lead weight, surmounted by a chip-carved gilt bronze wolf's head. The eyes are inlaid with two green glass beads. At the back of the head there is a neat rounded cut where the piece would have originally continued forming part of a strap end.

V237
Solid triangular shaped lead "weight", surmounted by a chip-carved gilt bronze wolf's head.

CM

V238
Solid circular lead "weight" with an inset square-shaped fragment of a gilt chip-carved strap fitting.

CM

V238 is a solid circular lead weight with an inset square-shaped fragment of a gilt chip-carved strap fitting. The design is of lozenges with a flattened edging on two sides.

V239 is a solid circular lead weight with an inset gilt bronze disc with a fantastic animal. This is based on a styca design.

V239
Solid circular lead "weight" with an inset gilt bronze disc with a fantastic animal.

CM

V240 is a solid rectangular lead weight with an inset glass blue and white glass bead of millefiori design.

The inset pieces vary considerably in weight and from examination of other published examples, numbering 28 in total, they have a range of weights from 1.8gm to 114gm. No two weigh the same, although there are groupings between 2.9gm to 3.9gm, 8.8gm and 9.8gm, 22.9gm and 24.4gm, and also between 38gm and 40.6gm. This does compare to the *ortugar* spherical bronze weights discussed earlier. However, an example set with an Alfred the Great penny weighed 24.2gm, while an example set with a King Burgred penny weighed 10.6gm. It is worth bearing in mind that lead oxidises over time and that inconsistency of weight is to be expected. This could be both as an increase in weight due to crystallisation, or a decrease due to corrosion.

V240
Solid rectangular lead weight with an inset of millefiori glass.

CM

Gaming Pieces

Everyone is familiar with the game of chess, which arrived in Europe in the 7th century AD from the East. The game has been adapted and improved from its origins in the 6th century AD until it has evolved into its present form. The most famous early surviving chess pieces were found in 1831 in the Outer Hebrides on the Isle of Lewis. They were made from walrus ivory and number 78 in total, presumably from different sets. They date from the 11th or 12th century. The design of these chessmen is similar to the modern day sets with figures representing the pieces. Earlier sets are often non-representational as the Muslim religion prohibits images of living creatures.

The game of chess has many distantly related board games, some of which involve dice and different playing boards. One of these is the game of "Hnefatafl" which translates into English as "The King's Chequered Table". The name is an old Norwegian word and can be pronounced in two ways, either "hen-af-tale" or "nafle-tafle". In the Oslo Museum are the remains of a wooden board and some counters made of bone. Additionally, in Ireland some counters of bone, glass or stone have survived. These are the only remaining original evidence of the game from the Viking era (8th-10th centuries).

The game was popular throughout Northern Europe during this period as the Vikings dominated the region. In Britain the game of "Hnefatafl" was popular and was last recorded as being played in Wales in 1587. By this time the game had changed from its original form and in fact, developed different forms of play in different countries. Very few gaming pieces have so far been found in Britain that could be associated with this game. **V241** is a possible example made in stone that was found in East Anglia.

A group of detectorists who search in Lincolnshire have found Viking objects and coins in an area of high ground bordered by two rivers. The coins date from the 8th and the 9th century comprising *stycas* and silver pennies. A quantity of fragmentary chip carved gilt-bronze artefacts together with a large quantity of lead weights also came to light. Some of the latter have been inset with coins or decorative chip-carved bronze pieces (see **V237-V240**).

From the Viking finds of lead weights in Lincolnshire only a very small number have been inset in this

V241
Stone gaming piece.

CM

V242
Arched and ribbed lead gaming piece.

CM

V243a
Hollow spherical
lead gaming piece.　　　CM

V243b
Hollow dome-shaped
lead gaming piece.　　　CM

V243c
Hemispherical
lead gaming piece.　　　CM

V244a
Hollow domed
with three projections
lead gaming piece.　　　CM

V244b
Solid domed
with four projections
lead gaming piece.　　　CM

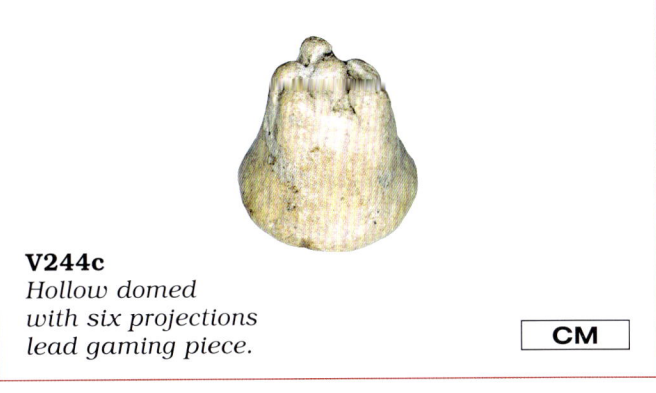

V244c
Hollow domed
with six projections
lead gaming piece.　　　CM

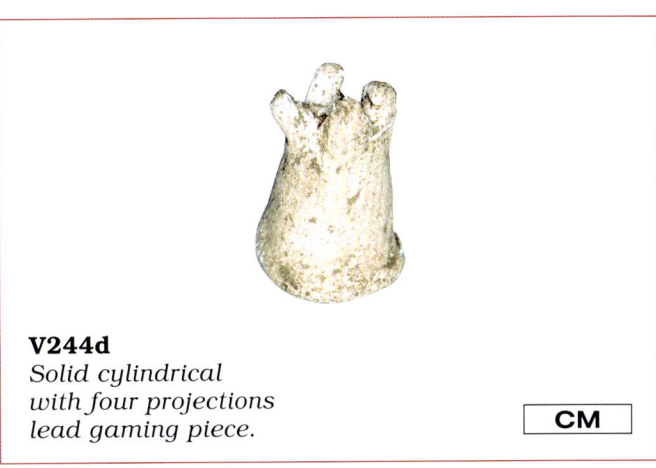

V244d
Solid cylindrical
with four projections
lead gaming piece.　　　CM

manner (approximately 13 out of 500). The remaining pieces all have a flat, often hollowed-out base, and are of varying shapes. The most common is dome-shaped, sometimes with a nipple on the top and sometimes with raised ribs forming a cross at the top (see **V242**, and **V243a, b, & c**).

It is these pieces that may have been used for gaming pieces rather than as weights. This suggestion is based on the inconsistency of weight between the pieces, the fact that almost 50% are hollow, and the sheer quantity found. Of 50 randomly selected undecorated "weights", only two weighed the same. The weight varied from 5.4gm up to 119.7gm, while the main area was in 10.6gm to 17.5gm range.

The variety of shapes found may have some relation to their use as gaming pieces. A small percentage have projections at the top (see **V244a, b, c, & d**). These vary from three to six in number, and have the appearance of a modern-day rook or castle chess piece. Inconsistency of weight was also noted ranging from 5.5gm to 26.3gm. The numbers of projections do not indicate an average increase in weight.

How The Game Was Played

Fig18

The game of Hnefatafl was played between two players on a wooden board marked out into 121 equal squares, arranged in 11 horizontal and 11 vertical rows. In the centre of the board sits the king on a special square signifying a castle. Around him are placed 12 defensive pieces (see Fig18). The attacking pieces are arranged around the edges of the board in formations of six on each side making a total of 24. As you can see from the photograph, the defensive pieces have projections while the attacking pieces are domed. This suggestion is based on the relative quantities that have been found in Lincolnshire.

The purpose of the game for the defence is to place the king in one of the corner squares, which are also designated as castles. The purpose of the game for the attacker is to surround the king on all four sides preventing him from moving.

Each piece moves in straight lines the same as a rook or castle in chess. The attacker always moves first, followed by the defence and then alternately. The pieces may be moved in any direction except diagonally, and for as many squares that are not occupied by another piece. Pieces may not jump over another, but they can jump over the centre castle square if it is not occupied by the king. Only the king is allowed to occupy the space of the four corner castles.

A piece is captured and removed from the board when enemy pieces are placed on opposite sides of the opponent's piece (see Fig19). However, if a piece is moved between two enemy pieces already there it is not captured. A piece is also captured if it has a corner castle on one side and an opponent on the opposite square. The king can also be used by the defence to capture pieces, but cannot be removed from the board unless he is surrounded (see Fig20) or if he has the centre castle on one side, and opponents on each of the other three sides.

From my own experiments of playing the game, according to these rules, it is extremely difficult for the attacking player to win by capturing the king. It is far easier for the defence to open out the board and provide a safe passage for the king to reach one of his corner castles. This is intriguing because it means the

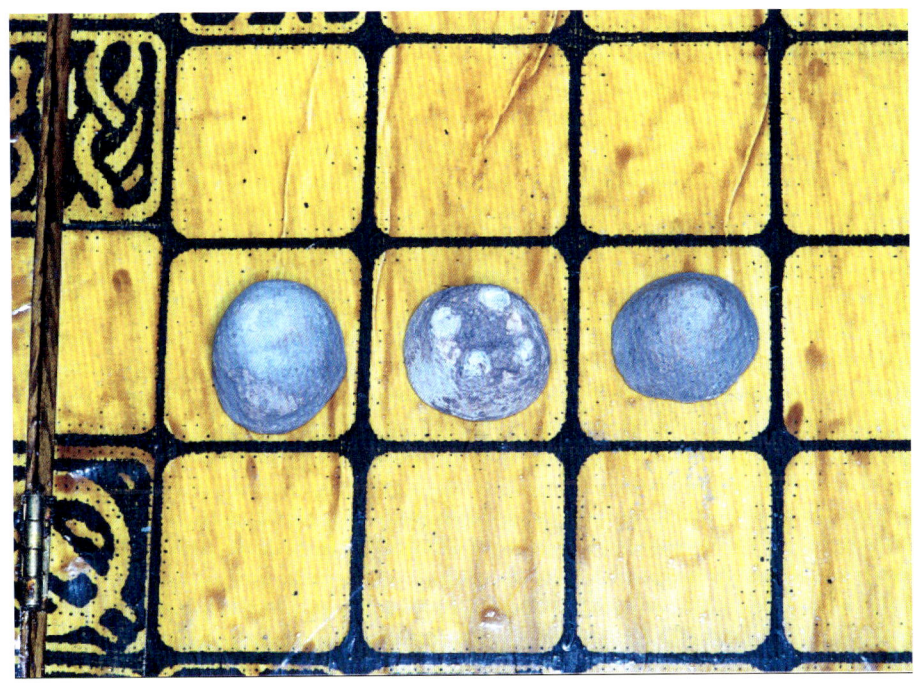

Fig19

Fig20

game is one-sided, and its purpose is to think of a strategy for the attacking team that outwits the defending team. Bearing in mind that the Vikings were essentially concerned with aggressive warfare, the game enabled them to think about the different dimensions on a battlefield in order to extract a victory.

Presumably each player would have taken turns in defence and attack, with no victory attached to a winning defence game as it is the most logical outcome. It is only when the king is captured that a victory has been achieved and that the stakes played for would be successfully won. The question is, was it a financial wager or would you quite literally lose your king piece? A successful player would amass a collection of king pieces. This would make sense if the pieces had some intrinsic value. This is where the inset and decorated lead "weights" could have a part to play. From the numbers that have been found in Lincolnshire the ratio of "king" to other pieces (approximately 1:36) is correct.

Another important aspect to the discovery of such a larger number of lead "weights" from such a small area is due to the fact that the Vikings had winter retreats or camps which would be located in safe areas and here it would be logical for them to be playing games etc during the resting period.

V245a
*Hollow domed
with expanded opening
lead gaming piece.*

CM

V246
*Hollow, arched,
central point and ridging.*

CM

V245b
*Solid with
central projection
and wide base.*

CM

There seem to be quite a number of different shapes and styles to these lead gaming pieces, and this may represent a long period of usage and also to differentiate between different sets. **V245a & b** and **V246** show some more examples. **V245a** is domed and hollow with an expanded opening. **V245b** is solid with an expanded base and central projection. **V246** is hollow with an arched top with central point and ridging around the sides (this piece could be a king). At present no clear representation of a king is known in England, although two carved examples of gods (possible king pieces) have been found in Scandinavia. A recent survey, conducted through **Treasure Hunting** magazine, has revealed a number of sites producing these gaming pieces in Lincolnshire and South Yorkshire. An inset weight was found in East Anglia with a gold zoomorphic head inset into the lead. This is the only known example.

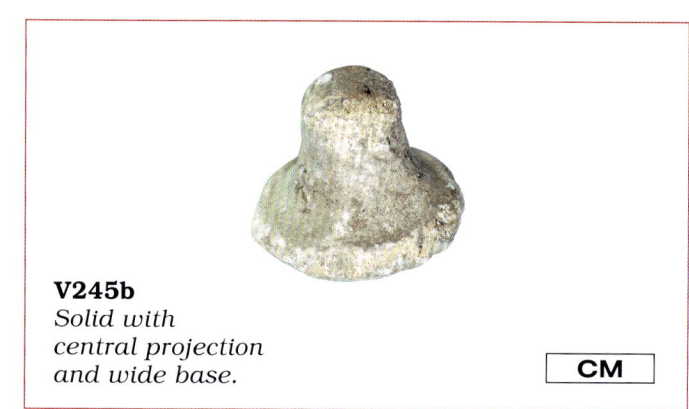

V245c
*Solid with central boss
and sloping expanded base.*

CM

Price Guide

Ref	Description	Fine	Very Fine
AS234	Bronze cube weight decorated with facemasks.	£300	£800
V235	Bronze plated iron sphere weight.	£75	£200
V236	Polyhedral bronze weight. (A complete matching set would be worth considerably more)	£12	£30
V237	Solid triangular shaped lead "weight", surmounted by a chip-carved gilt bronze wolf's head.	£150	£400
V238	Solid circular lead "weight" with an inset square-shaped fragment of a gilt chip-carved strap fitting.	£50	£125
V239	Solid circular lead "weight" with an inset gilt bronze disc with a fantastic animal.	£120	£350
V240	Solid rectangular lead weight with an inset of millefiori glass.	£35	£100
V241	Stone gaming piece.	£10	£20
V242	Arched and ribbed lead gaming piece.	£7	£15
V243a	Hollow spherical lead gaming piece.	£6	£12
V243b	Hollow dome-shaped lead gaming piece.	£7	£15
V243c	Hemispherical lead gaming piece.	£5	£10
V244a	Hollow domed with three projections lead gaming piece.	£8	£16
V244b	Solid domed with four projections lead gaming piece.	£8	£16
V244c	Hollow domed with six projections lead gaming piece.	£9	£18
V244d	Solid cylindrical with four projections lead gaming piece.	£9	£18
V245a	Hollow domed with expanded opening lead gaming piece.	£7	£14
V245b	Solid with central projection and wide base.	£6	£12
V245c	Solid with central boss and sloping expanded base.	£6	£12
V246	Hollow, arched, central point and ridging.	£10	£20

Runes

Runic script was a Germanic alphabet, probably based on Greek characters. It was originally called "Futhark" after the phonetic pronunciation of the first six letters. The numbers of letters in the Runic alphabet varied in different centuries; originally there were 24 letters but the Vikings used 16. There were two styles of representing the letters called long or short twig. The word rune means a "whispered secret" and is mentioned in Norse mythology when Odin - in his nine days and nights hanging from the Yggdrasill tree - seized the rune. The letters are not normally written but are inscribed or scratched onto wood, bone, stone, or metal. In Scandinavia there are many memorial stones with runic inscriptions. Sweden has the largest number of surviving runic inscriptions totalling 2,400. In Britain there are only 50 known examples, the majority of which are the names of the maker or owner of the object bearing the runes.

Key To Letter Coding

In order to indicate the period or origins of any particular item described in these pages a simple letter code preceding the illustration number has been used. A key to the meaning of these letter symbols is given below.

AS = Anglo-Saxon
Item manufactured by Germanic tribes in England but with a Celtic or native influence in the design. (AD 450-1066)

F = Frankish
Items manufactured on the Continent and imported into Britain by the migrating Frankish tribes, predominantly AD 410-500. The Franks were originally Teutonic people who advanced from Germany into France in the 5th century. Their influence waned by the middle of the 6th century.

M = Merovingian
Items manufactured by the Frankish dynasty that ruled Gaul during the 6th and 7th Centuries

V = Viking
(Items produced both in Scandinavia and in northern Britain between AD 793-1066 or with Scandinavian styles)

Chapter 10

Wrist-Clasps & Dress Hooks

The fastening of clothing in the 6th century was performed in three ways: using brooches, pins, and clasps. One specific style of clasp is referred to as a "wrist-clasp". These were worn in pairs on the garment adjacent to the sleeve and have been found in women's graves in England. From the large numbers recovered they were clearly very fashionable in the 6th century. The simplest form, such as the example shown as **AS255**, were made of thin sheets of rectangular bronze with a simple punched design of dots and grooves (repousse). They would have been stitched to the

Wrist clasps have generally survived from being discovered in situ in graves, along with brooches, pins, and other items associated with pagan burials. Therefore if you come across one of these it is a good indication of a burial in the vicinity that may have been disturbed by ploughing. Most Saxon graves are discovered at a depth of between 0.5m to 1m, which is very shallow compared to Roman burials.

Another similar pair of wrist clasps in cast form, **AS257**, both have scalloped outer edges with extended stitching loops. The thicker rectangular bar acts as a reinforcement, but also adds considerably to

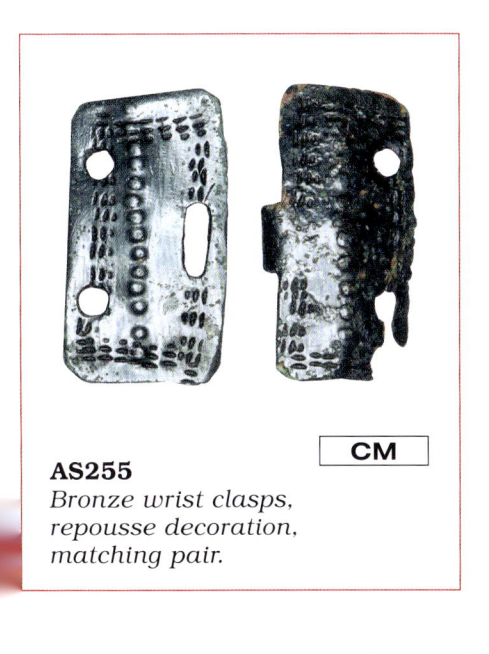

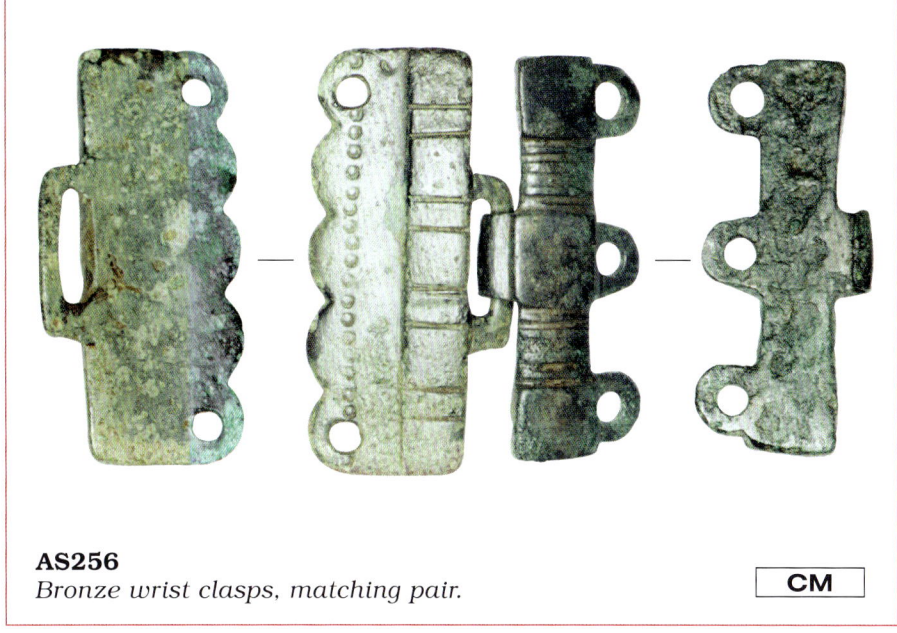

AS255
Bronze wrist clasps, repousse decoration, matching pair.

AS256
Bronze wrist clasps, matching pair.

clothing through the pairs of circular holes, and would have connected together through a turned-over hook, which fixed through an opening on its pair.

A more developed and robust pair of wrist clasps is shown as **AS256**. These are of cast bronze, again of rectangular form with stitching holes, which are often contained within projecting lugs. The hook is connected through an extended lug so that there is a gap between the two clasps. There is a simple decoration of grooves and ring and dot pattern. From the different form of the two clasps this is not an original matching pair although they were found in close proximity to each other.

AS257
Bronze wrist clasps, matching pair.

AS258
Bronze wrist clasp, chip-carved design. CM

AS260
Gilded bronze wrist clasp, chip-carve design. CM

AS261
Gilded bronze wrist clasp, chip-carved design. CM

the weight. It is again decorated with grooves and rectangular panels.

Another wrist-clasp is **AS258**. This has a chip-carved design with two animal heads and the surface has traces of gilding. It is of quite heavy fabric with a single stitching or rivet hole, and an extended rectangular lug for receiving the hook. A pair of wrist-clasps are shown in **AS259**. Again the design is chip-carved with a considerable amount of gilding remaining. Each half has a pair of animal heads and the overall design is more elaborate than on the previous example. The quality of these wrist-clasps indicates that they would have been worn by a fairly wealthy female.

The range of forms incorporating Style I Animal - even for a simple object such as a wrist-clasp are considerable and two further examples **AS260** and **AS261** show two different shapes, both chip carved and gilded. **AS261** has T-shaped extensions with square panels containing zoomorphic heads, while **AS260** has finer quality detailing and is T-shaped in overall form. It also has traces of tinning on the surface. Some female garments had an additional bronze plate fitted on the sleeve above the wrist-clasp; these are called gusset-plates. **AS262** is a beautiful example of a heavily gilded type, of extended triangular form, with a facing animal head with large circular eyes and a rectangular extension from the mouth. A pair of animal heads is also present on each side and at the top. The mouths enclose a rivet or stitching hole. The necks of the animals have punched triangles and also circles, and there may have been a garnet mounted in the centre recess. This also dates from the 6th century.

AS259
Bronze wrist clasps, gilded chip-carved design, matching pair. CM

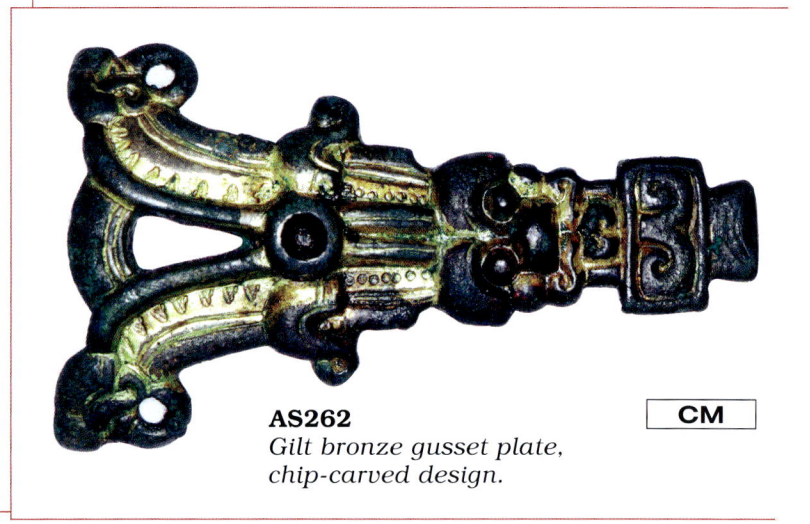

AS262
Gilt bronze gusset plate, chip-carved design. CM

Dress Hooks

The use of hooked tags for fastening first became fashionable during the Anglo-Saxon period. They are usually triangular or circular in shape, of sheet metal (normally bronze but occasionally silver), and have two or three attachment holes at the widest end.

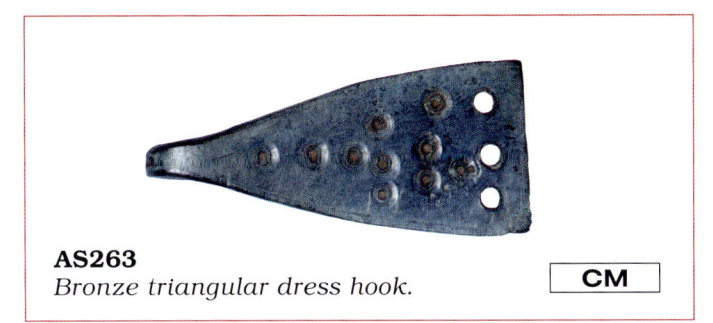

AS263
Bronze triangular dress hook.

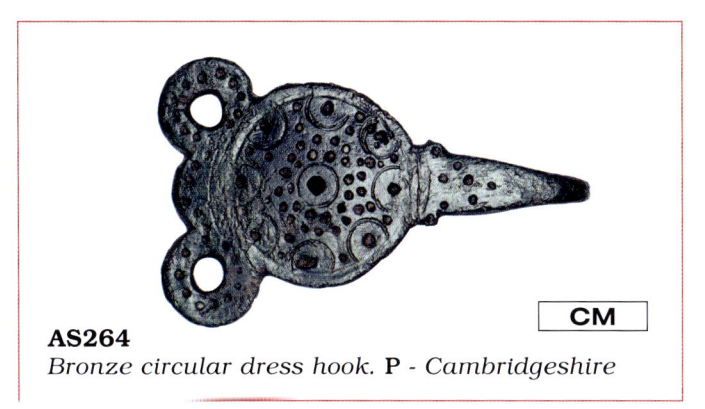

AS264
Bronze circular dress hook. P - Cambridgeshire

AS263 is a simple example of a triangular shape with three perforations at the top, and a turned over hook at the opposite end. The surface is decorated with a series of haphazard ring and dot punches. A similar example was found at Coppergate in York dating from the late 9th century. The archaeological evidence suggests that these hooked tags were in use from the 7th century and then in continuous use until the end of the medieval period. This I believe to be incorrect. Hooked tags were in primary use in the 9th and 10th centuries, especially during the Viking occupation and then fell into disuse until the Tudor period (c1520-1600). During this time they become very ornamented, usually with applied floral motifs, and are of heavier construction with an additional fixing plate situated underneath instead of the attachment holes. At this time they were primarily used for attaching ladies' scarves - one at the back and presumably one at the front (see Briegel's painting "The Wedding Party" c1580).

The Anglo-Saxon hooked tags have been referred to as "garter hooks" because some have been found in graves by the knees of the interred body. Others, however, have been found around the region of the head and the waist. A possible suggestion has been made that these were used as fixings for a funerary shroud. From their flimsy construction they must have been used for a light fabric. It is curious, however, that a similar device re-emerged in Tudor times.

The most common of the Anglo-Saxon dress hooks are circular with two lobes containing the attachment holes. **AS264** is a fine example in bronze with a series of dotted punches combined with an outer border of ring and dots. Again this is likely to date from the 9th century.

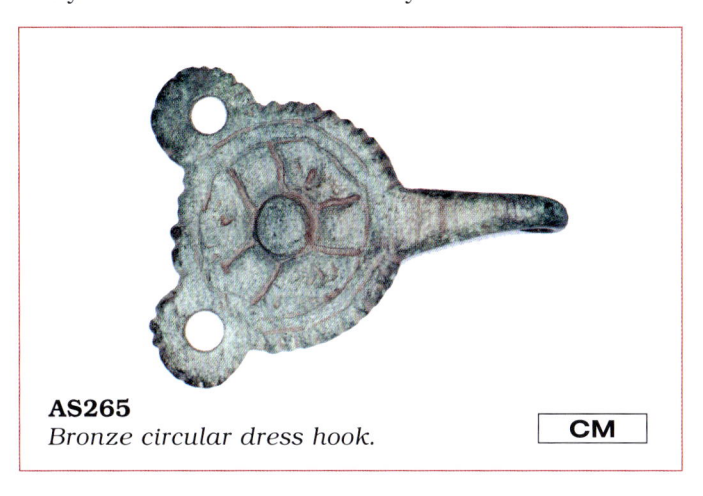

AS265
Bronze circular dress hook.

Another more-simple version, **AS265** has a raised boss in the centre. It is again of circular form, with the main panel divided into three segments by incised grooves. The outer edge is incised creating a scalloped effect.

AS266
Bronze triangular dress hook, quadruped decoration.

It is interesting to note that some of the dress hooks are influenced directly from the strap ends of the late 9th century. **AS266** is triangular in form with a zoomorphic terminal. The central panel has a quadruped with an interlaced ribbon design. There is a beaded edge and the eyes of the animal are inset with glass.

AS267
Bronze circular dress hook. CM

An interesting circular dress hook shown as **AS267** has a floral motif with eight segments and a central knot; it is probably 10th century in date.

AS268
Bronze and niello dress hook. CM

Some of the bronze dress hooks are decorated with niello inlay. **AS268** has a cross design outlined in niello. It is of oval form with four lobes and two small attachment holes at the top.

AS269
Silver circular dress hook. CM

Examples of dress hooks in silver are rare and very difficult to find undamaged as the silver hooks are prone to breakage. **AS269** is a circular type with very simplistic interlaced bands forming a cross pattern. The attachment holes have been punched within the circular frame. The hook is elongated and may have been stretched out as a result of use.

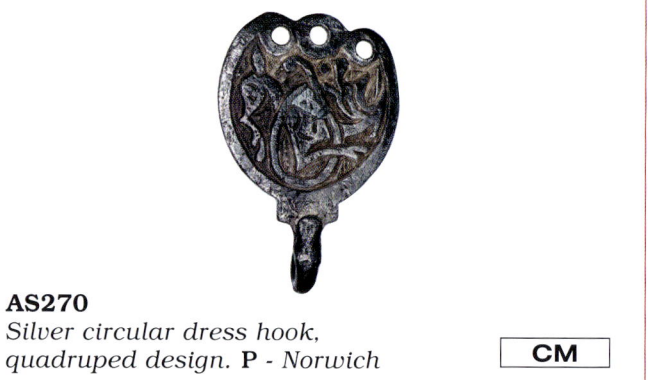

AS270
Silver circular dress hook, quadruped design. **P** - *Norwich* CM

AS270 is a quite elaborate circular dress hook with a reinforced, thickened hook. The central design has a quadruped with its head turned back. The field would have been originally inset with niello. There are three attachment holes, and this - combined with the thickened hook - gives it a more robust appearance.

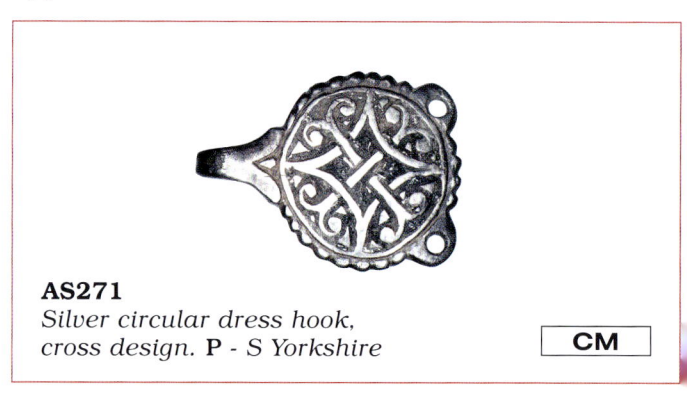

AS271
Silver circular dress hook, cross design. **P** - *S Yorkshire* CM

Another circular silver example **AS271** has the attachment holes mounted on extended lugs, a scalloped border, and a central panel of a lozenge with an interlaced cross. The hook has a floral design at its junction with the plate. This example would date to the 10th century and the design may be of the Winchester School.

Price Guide

		Fine	Very Fine			Fine	Very Fine
AS255	Bronze wrist clasps, repoussé decoration, matching pair	£12	£25	**AS263**	Bronze triangular dress hook.	£6	£15
AS256	Bronze wrist clasps, matching pair	£16	£35	**AS264**	Bronze circular dress hook.	£9	£22
AS257	Bronze wrist clasps, matching pair	£15	£32	**AS265**	Bronze circular dress hook.	£6	£15
AS258	Bronze wrist clasp, chip-carved design.	£18	£45	**AS266**	Bronze triangular dress hook, quadruped decoration.	£35	£110
AS259	Bronze wrist clasps, gilded chip-carved design, matching pair.	£140	£350	**AS267**	Bronze circular dress hook.	£7	£18
AS260	Gilded bronze wrist clasp, chip-carve design.	£60	£140	**AS268**	Bronze and niello dress hook.	£7	£20
AS261	Gilded bronze wrist clasp, chip-carved design.	£18	£45	**AS269**	Silver circular dress hook.	£25	£60
AS262	Gilt bronze gusset plate, chip-carved design.	£180	£425	**AS270**	Silver circular dress hook, quadruped design.	£110	£275
				AS271	Silver circular dress hook, cross design.	£65	£160

Dimensional Scales

The majority of objects illustrated in this book have been photographed alongside a CM (centimetre) scale. Most small artefacts are 150%, while larger objects are shown 100%.

Provenance

P = Find site of artefact

Sword & Scabbard Fittings, Knives & Weapons

Chapter 11

The most important possession for a Saxon warrior was his sword. Made of iron and usually between 84-90cm in length, it was a status symbol that was often passed down through generations. The finest blades were made by the Franks in Germany, using a process known as pattern welding. Iron rods and flat bars of different thickness and alloys were twisted and forge welded together, forming a pattern that was visible on the surface of the polished metal. The process was specialised and complicated, but made the sword blade extremely robust while the pattern (usually herringbone) - visible on the surface - revealed the quality of the sword. Pattern welding declined in the 9th century, probably due to finer quality iron ore being discovered and used. In some cases swords had steel blades but these were never put into pagan burials. Swords of this quality would have been highly decorative and even given a name such as Arthur's Excalibur. From pagan burials in Britain it has been estimated that a sword is found in one out of 20 male graves. The sword was placed at the side of the body, generally in its scabbard.

Anglo-Saxon swords normally had a double-edged blade and were a slashing weapon. Some have a central groove, which is called a fuller, running down the blade. This helped to strengthen the blade and also reduced the weight. The main differences that occur with swords is in the shape and decoration of the hilt. In the late 6th and 7th centuries hilts were of a composite wood and metal design. The wood was riveted between the diamond or triangular-shaped pommel and a flat fixing bar. The grip would have been made of horn, and the iron hand guard was straight.

AS272 shows a bronze sword pommel dating from the late 5th century. It is sub-triangular with a rounded top. The central panel is decorated with ring and dot punches and on each side of this are bands of vertical grooves.

AS273 is again sub-tr[i]... shape and may date to ... th... century. It is bronze ...ded surface, a few traces ...ing in the recesses. T[h]... carved and takes ... n ... wo back-to-back scrolls. Th[e i]ron tang at the end of the blade would have been inserted through the centre opening in the pommel; the iron tang was then hammered over to stop the handle from slipping off.

AS273
Gilt bronze sword pommel. **P** - *Suffolk* CM

The other commonly found shape of pommel is referred to as being of "cocked-hat" style.

A number of sword pommels found in Kent and dating mid to late 6th century have a ring attached to one side. These resemble tiny finger rings and are usually decorated. They appear to have had no practical function and one suggestion has been that they may have been used to indicate allegiance to a king.

During the 7th century the hilt of a sword became recognised as a symbol of royal power. The Sutton Hoo burial contained a gold pommel and scabbard fittings. **AS274** shows part of a magnificent sword pommel dating from the early 7th century. On each side is an interlaced zoomorphic design in Style II (see "Styles of Art" page 10). Snake-like creatures are depicted with long and thin ribbon-like bodies. An applied band of filigree work forming pellets runs along the centre of each animal, with a finer border of filigree pellets forming the outline. These side sections

AS272
Bronze sword pommel. CM

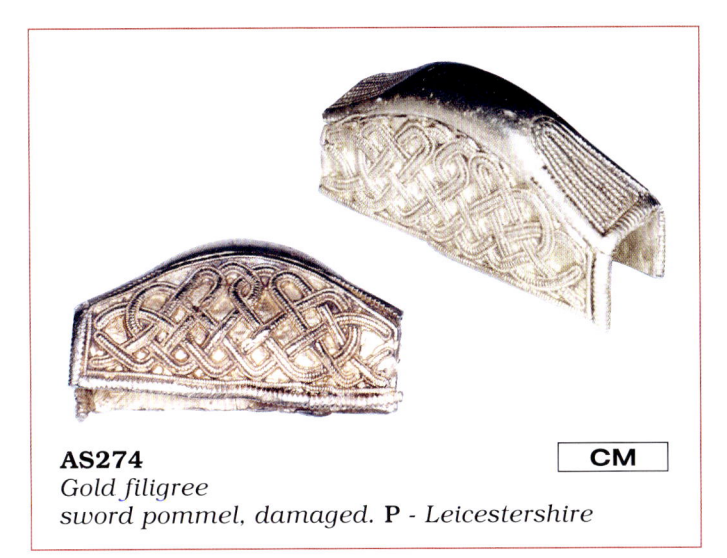

AS274
Gold filigree sword pommel, damaged. **P** - *Leicestershire*   CM

were soldered to the upper curved plate, which is decorated on each side with bands of twisted filigree wire. The end panels are missing, but would also have been decorated. The remains of this pommel represent the upper cap that was riveted at the side to a lower plate, in turn fixed to the iron sword end. Pommels of this nature have been found in Viking treasure hoards in Scandinavia but with no traces of any sword remaining. Many of them are profusely and lavishly decorated with garnets. These pommels may be presentation pieces from a tribal king to honoured warriors, especially after a successful battle. They could also have been an indication of rank and not just of wealth.

From the 9th century bronze or silver pommels were usually three or five lobed with a high central panel. The divisions between the lobes are quite deep. In the late 9th century pommels and guards develop acute curves. In the 10th and the 11th centuries this developed into two facing crescents, so that the guard is curved downwards while the pommel curves upwards. The sides of the guard and pommel may be inlaid with silver zoomorphic decoration.

The Viking sword was slightly shorter at 70-80cm long than the Saxon types. The majority were double edged, with only a few given a single edge. Some were pattern welded while the later blades are inlaid with inscriptions indicating the maker and the name of the sword.

Swords of this period had quite small grips. This is not to suggest that the Vikings had small hands, but that when the sword was in use the hand overlapped the guard and the pommel.

One very interesting pair of mounts excavated from the Sutton Hoo ship burial, were found close to, and at either side, of the sword hilt. These were two gold pyramid mounts, each heavily inlaid on all four faces with garnets. The function of these mounts is entirely unknown, but they have been found in significant numbers all over the country made from bronze, gilt bronze, silver gilt, and gold.

AS275
Bronze pyramid mount. **P** - *Kent*   CM

One of the simplest examples is shown as **AS275a**. This is a tall hollow pyramid in bronze with a square foil-backed garnet mounted at the apex. The sides are all plain and there is no trace of any gilding. A view of the underside **AS275b** shows the straight bar across the hollow base. This would have been for a cord to attach the mount to a sword scabbard.

AS276
Silvered bronze pyramid mount.   CM

Another example, also in bronze but this time with silvering applied to the surface, is shown as **AS276**. This is a much shorter pyramid with a wider base. At the apex there is again a square foil-backed garnet, while each of the four sides has an incised border with three incised triangles at the base and an inverted triangle at the top.

AS277
Silver gilt pyramid mount.   CM

AS277 is a pyramid mount in silver with recessed side panels that have been gilded and chip carved. The panels carry a simple zoomorphic design that contains horseshoe-shaped serpents on two opposite sides and triangular shapes on the other sides. There is no setting for a garnet at the apex, which could be an indication that none were available when the mount was made. This suggests a mid 7th century date.

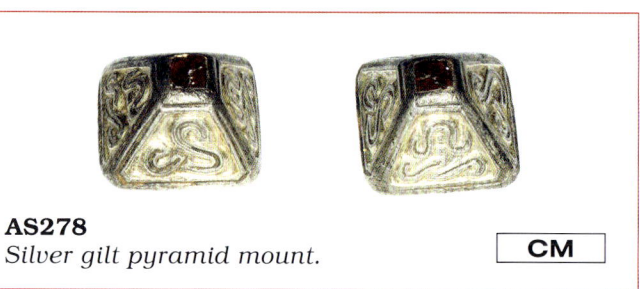

AS278
Silver gilt pyramid mount. **CM**

AS278 is another silver gilt pyramid mount, again with a wide base and shortened height. It has a square hatched, foil-backed garnet at the apex. As can be seen from the two views, the chip carved designs on each side are diametrically opposed. On each pairing of these is a different Style II interlaced design of simple form. The centre of each animal is recessed to receive niello inlay, most of which is now missing. The use of the interlaced design indicates a date from the early 7th century.

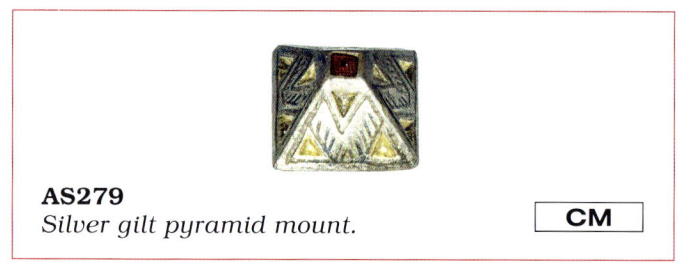

AS279
Silver gilt pyramid mount. **CM**

V280
Bronze sword chape, Borre style. **P** - *Yorkshire* **CM**

Another silver gilt pyramid mount is **AS279**. Similar to the previous example, it has a square hatched, foil-backed garnet at the apex. Each of the sides is decorated with three gilded triangles divided by a chevron with niello divisions.

Other gold pyramid mounts (see **AS274**) were probably made to match a sword pommel, and carry filigree interlace Style II ornamentation. It is believed that anything from one to three of these mounts would have been mounted either to the sword scabbard or to the sword itself. They could have been a follow-on from the earlier rings used on pommels in Kent to denote loyalty. Alternatively, they could have served as an indication of rank or status.

The fact that they all are of pyramid shape could indicate that they were thought to possess magical qualities, and thus give protection to their owner. The garnet at the apex could have been used as a healing stone. They appear to date from the late 6th to the mid 7th centuries. Their demise could be linked to the rise of Christianity.

Sword scabbards were made from wood lined with leather and wool, which contained lanolin to help prevent the rusting of the iron blade. The bottom of the scabbard was fitted with a bronze chape. The chape shown as **V280** dates from the early 10th century and has an interlaced zoomorphic design in the Borre style with a triple strand ribbon-like body. At the top is a triangular-shaped head, which has oval ears and a rounded nose.

V281
Bronze sword chape openwork design. **P** - *South Humberside*

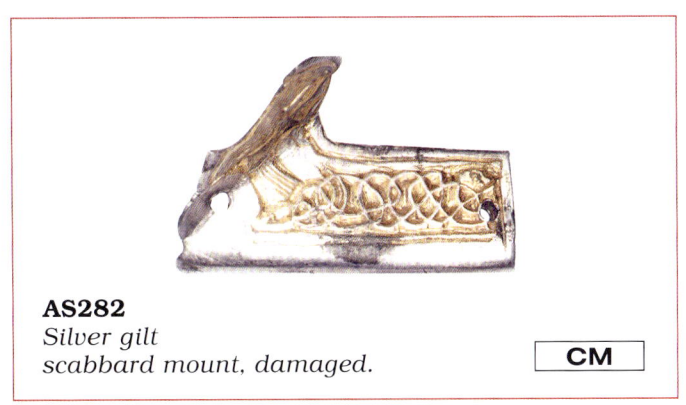

AS282
Silver gilt scabbard mount, damaged.

Another bronze chape, **V281**, is of openwork design with a human figure represented in the centre. It has a mask-like face with round eyes, crescent-shaped ears, and with limb-like projections around the body. This would again be 10th century in date.

AS282 is a silver gilt mount that was likely to have been riveted to the top or side of a scabbard. It has an interlaced design, which dates it to the late 8th century.

Apart from a sword, Anglo-Saxon warriors would have carried a shield and spear. The spearhead is the most common weapon found in graves, and was of iron with an ash or hazel shaft. In pagan burials the spear is normally positioned to one side of the skull, usually in a slightly higher position in the ground. **AS283** is a small example with an angular blade, and dates to the 6th century. The blades can also be leaf-shaped and quite long, such forms dating from the 6th and 7th centuries.

From excavations of pagan cemeteries it has been found that the younger the male, the shorter the spear. The range of size for the spearhead varies from 14cm to 48cm. It is logical that adolescent boys would have been equipped with short spears, because such spears would have been easier to throw. A heavy long spear was more of a thrusting weapon in hand to hand combat, and would have required strength and expertise to handle, which clearly limited them to adults. Viking spearheads are generally between 20cm to 60cm in length. In the 10th century the blades had long sockets and ridges while in the 11th century they were of heavier construction.

Anglo-Saxon shields were made from various woods: willow, popular, alder, birch and ash have all been identified. A circular iron boss (see **AS284**) was fitted to the centre of the shield, with an iron grip riveted behind. This took the form of a hollowed-out dome (to give space and protection to the hand) with an incurved waist with a wide flange, and four disc headed iron rivets with silver foil tops. In the centre of the dome is a projection, which is referred to as a "button" top. This boss dates to the 6th century.

There are several varieties of shield bosses - some have a spike projection, others have a narrow

AS283
Iron spearhead (rarely found in stable condition)

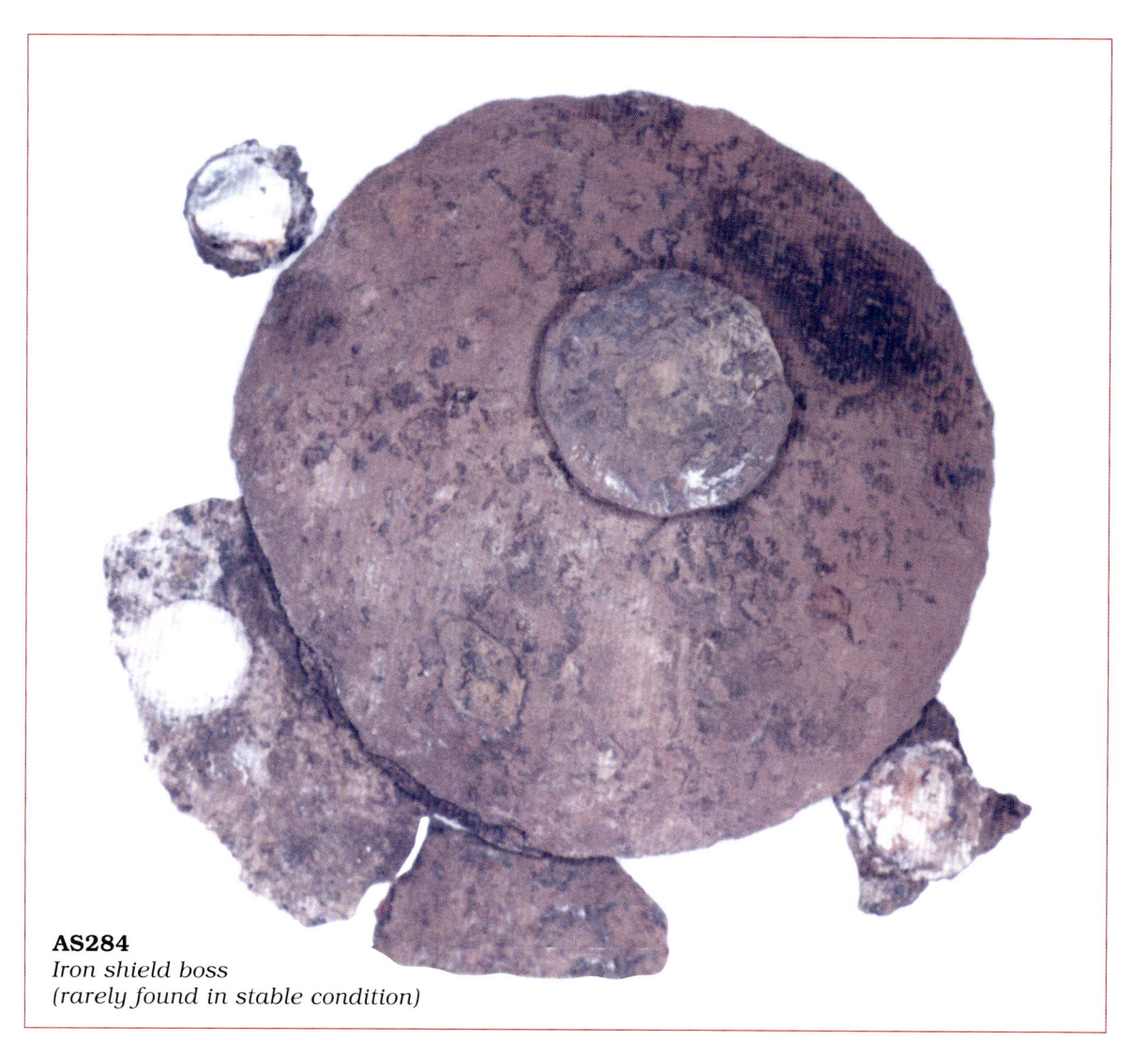

AS284
*Iron shield boss
(rarely found in stable condition)*

flange (which dates them to the late 6th century), and a few are quite tall in appearance, which may indicate a higher status for their owner.

On some shield bosses the central flat projection would have been capped with a decorated mount. **AS285** is an example of a chip-carved gilt bronze circular mount of the right size and date for a shield boss. It has a zoomorphic decoration around the outside in Style I, which gives it a date of the early 6th century. In the centre is a circular boss with radial lines around it. It shows two piercings in the outer field suggesting re-use as a pendant.

The Viking warrior carried a sword, shield and spear together with a battle-axe and a long knife called a sceax by the Anglo-Saxons. There were two forms of axe: a bearded hand axe and a curved headed throwing axe (which is called a Francasca). One distinctive feature of many Viking axes found in Britain, is that the iron is cold hammered to reduce it to a thinner gauge. This would have made the weapon lighter to carry but stronger in use.

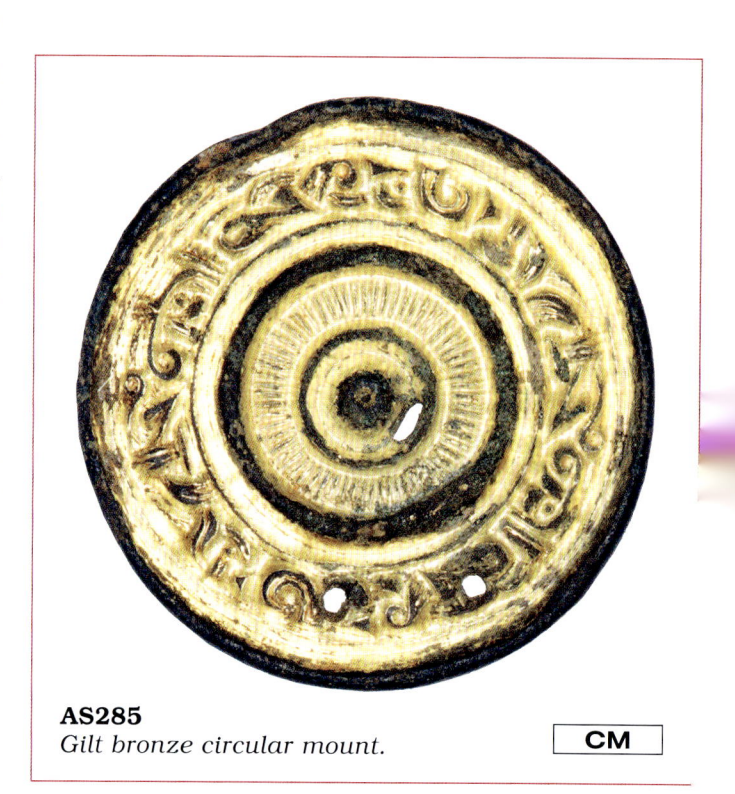

AS285
Gilt bronze circular mount.

CM

Knives

Scramasax is a Frankish name given to the robust single-edged iron knife of the Anglo-Saxon period. **AS286** is an example with a thickened back and a straight cutting edge. There is a sharp angle from the back to the tip of the blade. This form dates 9th-11th centuries, with the example illustrated probably dating to the 10th century. At this time bronze or silver inlay was often set into one side of the blade at the top edge. **AS286** has a coiled silver wire inlay forming two ridges, between which is a deep groove. Beneath the lower ridge are a series of seven semi-circular patterns of silver wire inlay. Some of these knives can be richly ornamented, with the design including the name of the maker and/or the owner.

In the Anglo-Saxon pagan period iron knives had a curved back, but by the end of the 7th century this had evolved into a straight back. Unfortunately, very few of the knives recovered from pagan burials have survived in a stable condition.

AS286
Iron scramasax knife blade with silver inlay. **P** - London

CM

Price Guide

		Fine	Very Fine			Fine	Very Fine
AS272	Bronze sword pommel.	£30	£75	**V280**	Bronze sword chape, Borre style.	£250	£600
AS273	Gilt bronze sword pommel.	£45	£120	**V281**	Bronze sword chape openwork design.	£175	£400
AS274	Gold filigree sword pommel, damaged. (Price range £1,500-£6,000. Complete examples have not come up for public sale).			**AS282**	Silver gilt scabbard mount, damaged. (Price range £40-£200).		
AS275	Bronze pyramid mount.	£40	£110	**AS283**	Iron spearhead (rarely found in stable condition)	£40	
AS276	Silvered bronze pyramid mount.	£45	£130	**AS284**	Iron shield boss (rarely found in stable condition)	£35	
AS277	Silver gilt pyramid mount.	£125	£350	**AS285**	Gilt bronze circular mount.	£240	£600
AS278	Silver gilt pyramid mount.	£260	£650	**AS286**	Iron scramasax knife blade with silver inlay.	£75	£240
AS279	Silver gilt pyramid mount.	£220	£525				

Genealogical Chart of Norse Gods

Bolthorn A giant, grandfather of the god Odin.

Buri A giant, licked from the primordial ice by a cow. The other grandfather of the god Odin.

Bestla A giantess, mother of Odin.

Bor A giant, son of Buri but mother unknown. Father of Odin.

Ve Brother of the gods Odin and Vili, suspected of being one of the lovers of Odin's wife Frigg.

Vili Brother of the gods Odin and Ve. The three together are responsible for creating the first humans.

Odin Father and most important of all the Aesir (the 13 male gods associated with war, death and power). He is distinctive in having a single eye and is shown wearing a hat and cloak, and carrying a spear. He is accompanied by two wolfs (Freki and Geri), and two talking ravens (Hugin and Munin), who fly everywhere on his behalf. At Ragnarok (the end of the old world) he is swallowed by the wolf Fenrir.

Frigg Wife of Odin and queen of the Asynjur (female Aesir or godesses, eight in number).

Jord Giantess, mother of Thor, believed to be the daughter of Nott (night).

Baldr Second son of Odin, described as wise and beautiful. His demise at the hands of Loki heralds the beginning of the end of the gods at Ragnarok.

Nanna Wife of the god Baldr and daughter of Nep. Dies with grief at the death of her husband.

Forseti One of the gods who had powers of arbitration.

Sif Wife of Thor, beautiful with golden hair.

Thor Son of Odin, and killer of giants. He is the prince of and strongest of the Aesir. He kills the Midguard Serpent at Ragnarok. Thor has golden hair, carries a hammer called Mjollnir in iron gloves, and wears a belt of strength.

Jarnsaxa A giantess, regarded as one of the nine mothers of the god Heimdall.

Módi Son of Thor, who after Ragnarok will inherit his hammer.

Thrud Daughter of Thor, sister of Magni and Modi.

Magni Son of Thor and half brother of Modi.

Heimdall Is the watchman of the gods whose vision extends more than 100 miles. He is the son of nine mothers, who were perhaps the daughters of a sea giant.

Ask & Embla Ask (ash tree) and Embla (elm tree) were the first humans created out of two tree trunks by Odin and two companions.

Njord A fertility god or Vanir, father of Frey and Freyja.

Freyja Second most important goddess, married to Od, and symbolises love.

Frey A fertility god, usually shown with a huge phallus.

Laufey A giantess and mother of Loki, her name means "leaf island".

Sigyn Goddess and wife of Loki. She remained loyal to her husband when he was bound to a rock with a snake hanging over him dripping venom.

Loki A god who was cunning and evil. He was father of Fenrir and the Midguard Serpent. He was constantly creating problems for the other gods.

Angrboda A giantess, mother of Fenrir, the Midguard Serpent, and Hel.

Nari Son of Loki. He was torn to bits by a wolf and his entrails then used to bind his father Loki.

Vali Son of Loki, sometimes represented as a dwarf.

Hel Daughter of Loki ruler of the underworld.

Fenrir Son of Loki, and a wolf. He remains bound until Ragnarok when he swallows the god Odin.

Jormungand The Midguard Serpent, son of Loki.

GENEALOGICAL CHART OF NORSE GODS

Key
- Line of Descent (black)
- Male Consort (blue)
- Female Consort (red)

Njörd
— Freyja
— Frey

Búri — Bór — Bestla — Bölthorn

Bór & Bestla → Odin, Vili, Vé

Odin — Frigg (consort); Odin — Jörd (consort)
Odin & Jörd → Thor
Ask, Embla

Frigg & Odin → Baldr
Baldr — Nanna → Forseti

Thor — Sif (consort); Thor — Jarnsaxa (consort)
Thor & Sif → Thrud, Módi
Thor & Jarnsaxa → Magni
Heimdall

Loki — Laufey
Loki — Sigyn → Nari, Vali
Loki — Angrboda → Hel, Fenrir (wolf), Jörmungand (midguard serpent)

105

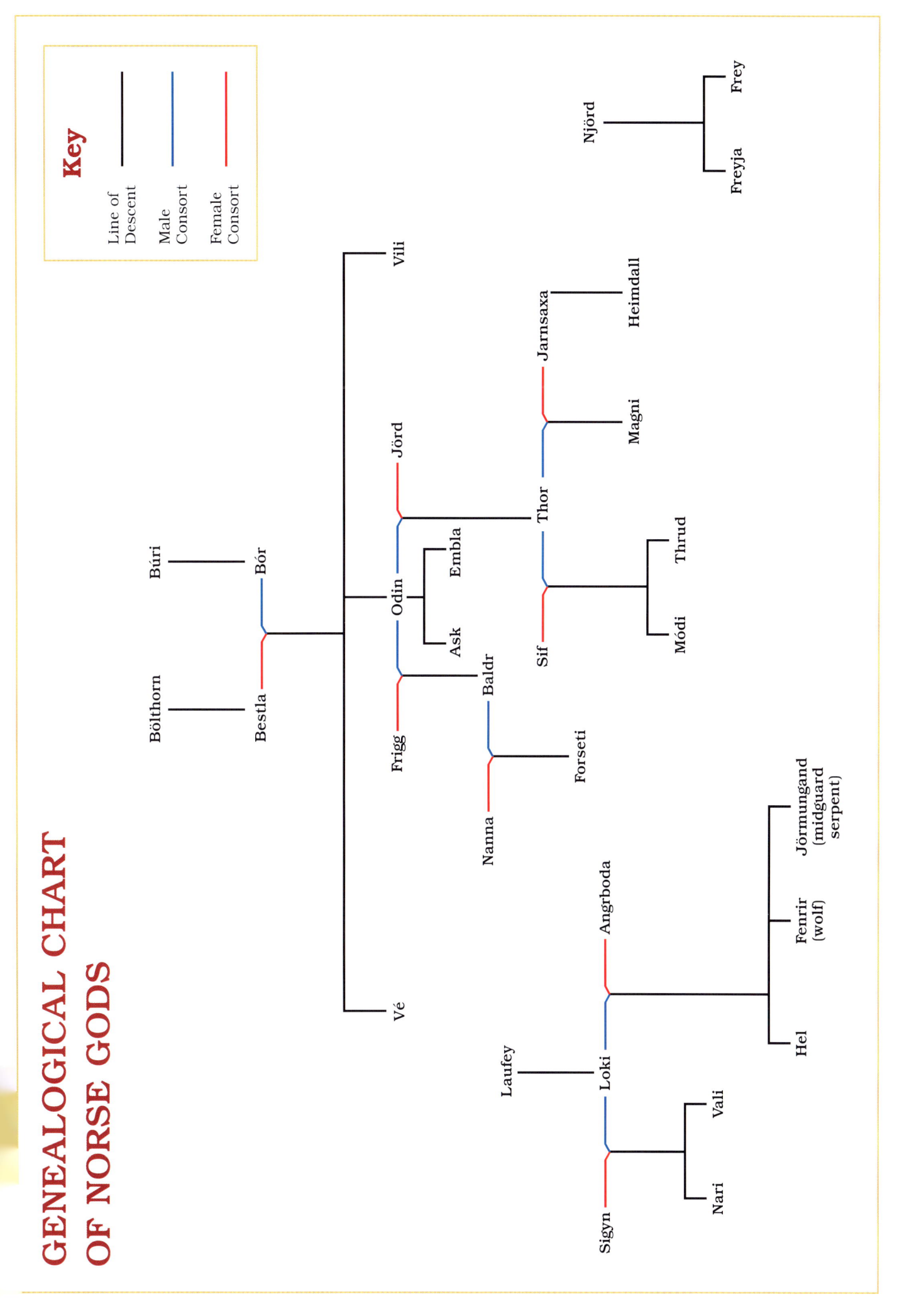

Select Bibliography

R. Avent	*Anglo-Saxon Disc & Composite Brooches* Parts I & II,	(BAR 11, 1975)
R. Avent & V. Evison	**Anglo-Saxon Button Brooches**	(Archaelogia 1982)
British Museum	**Guide To Anglo-Saxon Antiquities**	(1927)
British Museum	**The Making Of England - Anglo-Saxon Art & Culture AD 600-900**	(1991)
British Museum	**The Work Of Angels**	(1989)
CBA	*The Archaeology Of York - The Small Finds Vol 17 Fasc. 14 Craft, Industry & Everyday Life*	(2000)
Kevin Crossley-Holland	**The Penguin Book Of Norse Myths - Gods of the Vikings**	(Reprinted 1993)
H.E. Davidson	**The Sword In Anglo-Saxon England**	(Reprinted 1998)
V. Evison	*An Anglo-Saxon Cemetery At Great Chesterford, Essex*	(CBA Report 91, 1994)
V. Evison & P. Hill	*Two Anglo-Saxon Cemeteries At Beckford, Hereford & Worcester*	(CBA Report, 103, 1996)
David Haldenby	*Study of 9th Century Anglo-Saxon Strap Ends*	(Parts 1-3, **Treasure Hunting** magazine, December 1997, February 1998 and April 1998)
R. Hattatt	**Ancient & Romano-British Brooches**	(1982)
R. Hattatt	**Ancient Brooches & Other Artefacts**	(1989)
R. Hattatt	**Brooches Of Antiquity**	(1987)
R. Hattatt	**Iron Age & Roman Brooches**	(1985)
J. Hines	**A New Corpus Of Anglo-Saxon Great Square Headed Brooches**	(1997)
London Museum	**London & The Saxons**	(1935)
A. MacGregor & E. Bolick	*A Summary Catalogue Of The Anglo-Saxon Collection In The Ashmolean Museum In Oxford*	(BAR 230 1993)
C. Marshall	**Buckles Through The Ages**	(1986)
Museum of London	**Treasure & Trinkets**	(1991)
S. Margeson	*The Vikings In Norfolk* Norfolk Museum Service	(1991)
Nordic Council	**From Viking To Crusader - The Scandinavians & Europe 800-1200**	(1992)
Oslo	*The Viking Game - Hnefatafl*	(1995)
Oslo	**Viking Antiquities In Great Britain & Ireland Part VI**	(1954)
Oxbow	**The Pace Of Change - Studies In Early Medieval Chronology**	(1999)
Oxford University Press	*Anglo-Saxon Studies In Archaeology & History*	No.3. (1984), No.4. (1985), No.6. (1993), No.9. (1996)
P. Sawyer	**Oxford Illustrated History Of The Vikings**	(1997)
	The Vikings - The North Altlantic Saga Smithsonian Institute	(2000)
Richard Underwood	**Anglo-Saxon Weapons and Warfare**	(1999)
R. Whitehead	*Viking Metalwork In England* Parts 1 & 2,	(**Treasure Hunting** magazine February and May 1999)
D. Williams	*Late Saxon Stirrup Strap Mounts*	(CBA Report 111)
Michael Wood	**In Search of the Dark Ages**	(1981)